To Serve the Present Age

TO SERVE THE PRESENT AGE

*The Gift and Promise
of United Methodism*

J. PHILIP WOGAMAN

Abingdon Press
Nashville

TO SERVE THE PRESENT AGE
THE GIFT AND PROMISE OF UNITED METHODISM

Copyright © 1995 by Abingdon Press

This book is printed on recycled, acid-free paper.

Library of Congress Cataloging-in-Publication Data

Wogaman, J. Philip.
　To serve the present age : the gift and promise of United Methodism /
J. Philip Wogaman.
　　p.　cm.
　Includes index.
　ISBN 0-687-01711-4 (alk. paper)
　1. United Methodist Church (U.S.)　2. Methodist Church—United States.
　I. Title.
BX8331.2W64　1996
287'.6—dc20

95—46392
CIP

Scripture quotations are from the New Revised Standard Version Bible, Copyright © 1989 by the Division of Christian Education of the National Council of the Churches of Christ in the USA. Used by permission.

95 96 97 98 99 00 01 02 03 04— 10 9 8 7 6 5 4 3 2 1

MANUFACTURED IN THE UNITED STATES OF AMERICA

To Louise, Emily, and Carrie
Mothers in the Faith

Contents

Introduction

The title of this book, derived from a hymn of Charles Wesley, reminds us first and foremost that the church is called to serve. It does not exist for its own glory but to serve the everlasting will of God. It is called to serve in the present age, not because of its own choice, but because this is where God has placed it. There is a double meaning in Wesley's term, "the present age." On the one hand, age or *aeon* means now, this particular period of history in which we find ourselves. On the other hand, age or *aeon* means earthly existence in contrast to our eternal home with God. In any case, the church is here, present, in this part of history. And here it is we are called to serve.

But the church also has a past, and it reaches in anticipation toward a future. As I reflect upon United Methodism, I am almost overwhelmed by the immensity of the gifts it has been given in its little more than two hundred years of history. This book is structured around those gifts, emphasizing how the gifts also contain a promise for the future.

By referring to the "gifts" of United Methodism I am thinking of three forms of gifts: first, the gifts that have been given *to* this church through its origins and history—the church's legacy from the past; second, the gifts that the church offers now to its members and to the wider family of churches; third, the gifts that United Methodism offers to a troubled world as humanity completes the second thousand years of Christian history and enters the third.

While the title and the book are unabashedly about United Methodism, it is understood at the outset that this is not intended for the glory of one denomination in competition with others. We have had enough of that! Chapter 7 will explore the ecumenical gift of United Methodism, but it is clear that all denominations bring gifts. The denomination of which I write could not stand alone. Just as it offers its own gifts to the wider ecumenical church, so it gratefully receives the gifts of others. This denomination has not existed for all time, not even all Christian time. Nor, I am confident, will it exist forever in its present form. In God's good time it will blend its life into the broader stream, perhaps in ways we can scarcely imagine. I was born and raised a "Methodist," and I have never transferred my membership into another denomination. Nevertheless, there is a sense in which I have already belonged to three denominations: The Methodist Episcopal Church (before 1939), The Methodist Church (from 1939 to 1968), and The United Methodist Church (since 1968). The changes of status represented reunion and merger. Other United Methodists started their Christian journeys in other denominations before transferring to this one. I am sure that virtually every denomination, at least in the United States, has some presence of former United Methodists. So our gift is in and to a wider circle of Christian life and to a world that may extend beyond Christianity, but certainly not beyond the province and providence of God.

Still, I write as a grateful son of this denomination, and I wish to say some very personal things about that. I was born into a pastor's family in Ohio and grew up in a series of Methodist parsonages in small towns of Ohio and Arizona. I participated in vacation Bible schools, in the Methodist

Youth Fellowship, and in church summer camps—all of which were very important, along with family and local churches, in forming my identity as a Methodist Christian. I graduated from a United Methodist college (University of the Pacific) and seminary (Boston University School of Theology). I was called into ordained ministry in the (then) Southern California–Arizona Annual Conference, where I met my future wife, also a Methodist. We served briefly as missionaries before political developments in Cuba forced a change of direction. My doctoral dissertation was on Methodism's challenge and dilemma in race relations (1960). I taught Bible and ethics at a Methodist college (again, University of the Pacific) for five years, and I was on the faculty of a United Methodist seminary (Wesley Theological Seminary) for twenty-six years. During those years I was deeply immersed in the life and work of several local congregations. Though ordained, I participated essentially as a layperson, alongside other laypersons. I have served the church in one way or another on many organizational levels of its life, and I have experienced its vitality in many states of the United States and several other countries. For the past three years I have served as pastor of a United Methodist congregation.

I have been more richly blessed by such formative experiences on my own spiritual journey than I could hope to repay. I am deeply familiar with the church of which I write. In writing such a book I draw, of course, not only upon my own experience but also upon academic resources and the experiences of others. But this is not only an academic exercise. It is about and for a church that I love very much.

I am grateful to Ted A. Campbell, William A. Holmes, James C. Logan, Sally C. Mathews, William B. McClain, Walter Shropshire Jr., and V. Sue Zabel for reading an early draft of this manuscript and offering helpful suggestions and encouragement. While I must accept responsibility for the final form of the book, their criticisms have improved it, and

I am grateful. Sally C. Mathews has also provided invaluable secretarial assistance. I have shared most of my United Methodist pilgrimage with my wife Carolyn, whose companionship and encouragement in this as in all things contributes more than I can say.

To Serve the Present Age

Chapter One

THE GIFT OF GRACE

*T*his book is about gifts and promises—the gifts that have been given to us and the promises they represent for the future. The greatest gift of all, without question, is of God's grace, which we have received through Jesus Christ. That most important gift is not peculiar to United Methodism, but is shared with all other churches. Still, it is given to each in its own way. "In Christ God was reconciling the world. . . . " We may differ much in the way we have experienced this gift, but it is finally what we are all about.

How United Methodism Has Been "Graced"

How has United Methodism received this gift?

In the beginnings, in eighteenth-century England, it was given to figures like John and Charles Wesley, George White-field, the Countess of Huntingdon. It is difficult to place ourselves back in that time frame, to think and feel as people did then. The Industrial Revolution was just beginning. Many people were left out, many were exploited in coal mines and the earliest factories. Many had moved to cities, cutting ancestral ties, and then had been unable to find work.

It was a very corrupt age. Moral standards were loose; crime was on the rise, but ruthlessly punished (with hanging for what we might today consider fairly minor offenses). The established church was formal and reserved, both emotionally and socially. It was an age of comfortable religion, especially for the social and religious elite. Large numbers of people were, or felt themselves to be, left out. For common coal miners, or factory workers, or farmhands, or unemployed persons, it was easy to believe that they were of no account. They were looked down upon, and they looked down upon themselves. Such people were demoralized. They might have been overwhelmed by a sense of God's judgment upon them, but unable to feel anything of God's love.

The Wesleys' own upbringing contributed both to deep Christian commitment and profound spiritual insecurity. Like many Christians before them, they felt they had to earn God's favor with "good works," but they could never do enough. John Wesley became a missionary to colonial Georgia, spending two years ministering to the settlers and hoping to convert Native Americans. His ministry failed, largely because of his rigidities and a failed romance, and he returned to England. In January of 1738, a discouraged Wesley wrote in his *Journal*, "I went to America to convert the Indians; but Oh! who shall convert me? Who, what is he that will deliver me from this evil heart of unbelief?" (*The Works of John Wesley*, Volume 18 [Nashville: Abingdon, 1988], 211). Upon his return to England, Wesley's spiritual turmoil continued for several months until, on May 24, 1738, he had the experience that was to transform his life and the lives of countless followers:

> In the evening I went very unwillingly to a society in Aldersgate Street, where one was reading Luther's Preface to the Epistle to the Romans. About a quarter before nine, while he was describing the change which God works in the heart through faith in Christ, I felt my heart strangely warmed. I

felt I did trust in Christ, Christ alone for salvation, and an assurance was given me that he had taken away *my* sins, even *mine,* and saved *me* from the law of sin and death. (*The Works of John Wesley,* Volume 18, 249-250)

This experience and similar spiritual transformations in the lives of other early Methodist leaders were received as a pure gift of God. Wesley, his brother Charles, and others preached that gift of God's grace in Christ up and down eighteenth-century England, transforming the lives of thousands of people. From there the movement came to America where, in the eighteenth and nineteenth centuries, the gospel of God's grace spread like wildfire in the frontier outreaches of the new nation.

The history of Methodism in England and America is long, detailed, and interesting. But the heart of it, from the time of the Wesleys, has been the gift of grace—the deep sense that in spite of our unworthiness, God has said yes to us.

Meanwhile, we remember another great stream of grace that converged with Wesleyanism in 1968 when The Methodist Church and The Evangelical United Brethren Church merged to form The United Methodist Church. The heritage of the Evangelical United Brethren denomination, while different in detail, was similarly grounded in the gift of grace. Early leaders of what was to become The Evangelical United Brethren Church, Philip William Otterbein, Martin Boehm, and Jacob Albright received this gift through Mennonite and Lutheran heritages. Jacob Albright's experience was a bit like Wesley's:

I heard the voice of consolation in my soul. I . . . was convinced that since God does not desire the destruction of a sinner but that he should turn from his way and live, he would look upon my sincere repentance . . . with gracious eyes and that the merit of my Lord and his bitter suffering and death would complete the work. . . . God's spirit bore witness with my spirit that I was a child of God; one joyful experience followed another, and such a heavenly joy pervaded my whole being, as no pen can describe and no mortal can express. (In Raymond W. Albright, *A History of the Evangelical Church* [Harrisburg, Pa.: The Evangelical Press, 1956], 34-35)

The pietism of Albright and others, based upon the gift of grace, was the impetus for the founding of churches in America soon after the organization of Methodism.

This is the broad historical background. Perhaps more needs to be said to relate this to the ordinary experience of the tens of thousands of United Methodist churches across the United States and around the world. We may find it difficult to appreciate the significance of what happened to our spiritual forebears, such as the Wesleys and Albright, because of differences of cultural setting. But the gift of grace has continued to speak to people in this denominational tradition in formative ways. Most people who have grown up in the church can think of "graced" moments, such as the church school, in which devoted teachers give of themselves in the nurturing of young lives in the faith, accepting the children as they are, and illustrating with their own love the meaning of the faith they teach. I had church school and vacation Bible school teachers like that! Or the youth groups in which teenagers are encouraged to share their problems in an accepting and supportive environment. Or the church "covered-dish" suppers, to which all contribute and from which all receive. Or the moments of shared joy or shared grief or shared suffering, in which members reach out to one another instinctively to say or do the right thing to be channels of God's grace. No local church is perfect, but few, if any, are without the touches of grace that make our lives whole. We need to see grace in the ordinary ways in which it appears. We need to see it where we live and worship.

The church I serve is located in the heart of a great city. It is not in the most difficult neighborhood, but neither is it in the easiest. Here, one can literally encounter homeless people at the church's very doorstep and a congregation including persons of great power and influence worshiping alongside people of very modest means and influence. One is impressed by their common commitment to Christ and the church. After I had been here for a year or two and had got better acquainted with the people, I began to see why there was such loyalty. There are so many people who, in one way or another, have been wounded in their lives, sometimes unbelievably so. But they have found an acceptance through Christ and the love of fellow Christians that has enabled them to put their lives together again. Perhaps they have failed in some spectacular way. Perhaps they have suffered an extraordinary loss. Perhaps they have done an almost unforgivable injury to others. It takes something beyond our own resources to bring healing. And people who have found this through the church have a basis for deep loyalty. That is not commitment for the sake of commitment, nor is it based on a desire to prove anything to oneself or to God. It is a response to what God has done.

What Does Grace Mean to Us?

God's grace remains basic to everything else. What does it mean to United Methodists? We all have different ways of stating it, not least because we all experience grace uniquely and personally. For some, it has been a sudden, life-transforming moment when the assurance of God's love has come like a stroke of lightning—in a nineteenth-century camp meeting or revival, in a twentieth-century youth camp, or in some other setting. For others, it has been a slowly developing and deepening realization of the depth of God's love, nurtured by a caring family and loving church.

Common to all is the sense that God's love is not merited. We cannot claim to have earned it; it is freely given and received in faith. Common to all is recognition that we have received this gift through Christ. We will perceive this in different ways, too. But to speak of Christ is to remind ourselves that grace is not just an idea, not an abstraction. God's love can be expressed to us through Christ because Christ was both human and divine. Our faith is that the love of Christ, which we have seen and felt, is the love of God. And so we can say with I John 4:19 that "we love because he first loved us."

Despite our differences in ways of expressing this, grace has two very important implications for all of us. First, it means that there is absolutely no room for self-righteousness. We are all sinners, we are all imperfect, we are all dependent upon God's gift. That means we cannot think of ourselves as being better than other people. In a later chapter I will explore the church's role as a moral teacher and the fact that we have to struggle to apply Christian faith to the personal and social problems we face, and that is different from making judgments based on self-righteousness. Our shared need for God's grace means that there is no basis for human pretense.

The other implication is that we do not define ourselves on the basis of particular moral rules. There is a place for moral principles and rules, to be sure; the Methodist and Evangelical United Brethren traditions have given them great emphasis. But our life does not flow from them. Our life is transformed by God's grace, not by our conformity to specified rules. Paul is very clear about that. Even though Paul dealt with moral issues, sometimes in detail, he insisted that salvation comes through grace, not by what he called "works of the law." The meaning of this is that we are brought into the life of love; as we receive the gift of God's love, we ourselves also find it possible to love. Love is positive, overflowing. It is not a matter of conforming to rules. United Methodists, historically, have not always been as clear about that as our faith would suggest. Sometimes United Methodists have indeed defined themselves by what they don't do—for example, by giving the impression that a Methodist is primarily somebody who doesn't consume alcoholic beverages. Sometimes that is what we take spiritual "standards" to mean. But the roots of our faith are far more profound. The "standard" is God's grace and our loving response to God, God's creation, and fellow humanity. John Wesley was very clear about that: grace is prior to works. In this, he and the Methodist movement closely followed the emphasis of Luther and Calvin.

In historical Wesleyan theology, the priority of grace is recognized at every point in the Christian life. "Prevenient grace," for example, is taken to mean the grace that prepares the way. Typically, United Methodists have not been determinists. We do not, typically, believe that God has "elected" some to receive the gift of grace, but others not. Prevenient grace is understood as the anticipation—what goes before, enabling us to respond. Human love, for instance, might be considered a form of prevenient grace. "Justifying grace" is the grace providing us with the assurance of our salvation— that God accepts us, despite our unworthiness. It is this that Wesley experienced when he felt his heart "strangely warmed," and it is this that Christians experience as conversion (whether sudden or gradual).

Another peculiarly Wesleyan way to express what happens through grace is the doctrine of "Assurance." I'm certain this has its roots in Wesley's own spiritual struggle. He knew, theoretically, that salvation is through grace; he had a terribly difficult time *experiencing* it. There lurked in the background something of his semi-Calvinist upbringing through which one was always looking for evidences of one's salvation. Seen in that way, there can never be enough evidences, for there are always also evidences of one's continuing sinfulness. Wesley's conversion experience really came down to his breaking out of that box. He could feel the "assurance" that he really was saved. He could trust the God whom he met in Jesus Christ. "Sanctifying grace" is the steady nurturing love we experience that makes it possible for us to "grow in grace." When Wesley used the term "going on to perfection," he was not being abstract. Perfection meant being perfected in love.

The Promise of Grace

When United Methodists fully enter into this gift of grace in its different forms, they are caring in their treatment of one another and winsome in their witness to God's grace in the world. That witness is always needed. Times change, circumstances vary, the form of the message must be tailored to new occasions, but the message of grace is always both timeless and urgent. It is timeless because God is timeless and God's love is constant. It is urgent because there are always vast numbers of people whose lives are distorted by fear and the compulsion to find some substitute for real salvation.

When United Methodism ventures "to serve the present age," the greatest gift it has to offer is to be a channel of God's grace. In the closing years of the twentieth century, the world is clouded by mean-spirited, sometimes bloody conflict, by greed, by no small measure of self-righteousness, and always by the hurt loneliness of multitudes of people. Many of the specific symptoms are linked by the same underlying condition: we find it very hard to trust God's love, and therefore we find it doubly hard to let go in generous love for others. In various parts of the world there are religious and ethnic conflicts. Regardless of external form, what these wretched struggles come down to is people looking for salvation through their group identity, which must prevail at all costs. In many countries, not least in the United States, large numbers of people seek to find themselves by losing themselves to drugs and other forms of addiction. It does no good to condemn people for such unrighteous, self-destructive behavior. Mostly, they already know the emptiness of their addictions, the powerlessness of such temporary fulfillments to save. Addictions, whether of a chemical or a spiritual sort, have irresistible power unless challenged by the deeper power of love.

The appropriate response to such emptiness is not so much moralism as love—helping others to experience a deeper, positive meaning in life and a helping hand in the long, slow process of recovery—which could be called a form of sanctifying grace. Sometimes we resort to self-righteousness and vindictiveness in dealing with what we perceive to be the enemies of truth. But grace has to break through self-righteousness, and help us to see that God's gift of grace for each of us is also the basis of unity for all of us.

Jesus Christ, who manifests God's grace to us, is not uniquely United Methodist! But, together with all Christians, we proclaim with faith that, in the words of Paul, "In Christ God was reconciling the world to himself" (II Corinthians 5:19). And that, in the words of the Gospel of John, "From his fullness we have all received, grace upon grace" (John 1:16). That is the gift from which every other gift is derived. When United Methodists and other Christians offer Christ to the world, it is not in a spirit of arrogance or exclusivity. What is arrogant or exclusive about God's love? That love takes many forms, and its presence in our lives is unique to each of us, as well as common to all.

As we venture into the exciting world of a new century— and even a new millennium—is this not an extraordinary gift we have to share with the world? It would be spoiled if we let it be perceived only as our way of enhancing narrow institutional interests. The gift of grace needs to be expressed in institutional form, but it is bigger than the form, just as it is bigger than any of us. We must be prepared to serve that grace in unanticipated ways.

One night I was at a hospital in my city, visiting one of the members of my congregation and offering prayer. Afterward, long after visiting hours, I walked through the lobby downstairs. A distraught man called out to me in a foreign accent to ask where he might find the hospital chaplain. It was long after hours, I said, and the chaplain would have gone home. But I was a pastor; could I help him? Please, he said. His wife was in a coma upstairs dying. He wanted prayers to be said. He was Muslim, I was Christian, but still he wanted me to come. So we went up to the room, where his wife lay breathing her last troubled breaths, surrounded by a dozen or so loved ones who crowded into the room for this moment. I am not a Muslim, I said, but a Christian, but I cared for them as God cared for them. Which way is Mecca? I asked. The husband pointed in a precise direction, and I acknowledged this and the importance of it in their faith, for which I had respect. I said that God is here in this room, as well as Mecca, with which they agreed, and that God was there to care about them and their loved one. And so we prayed, they and I, that God would receive the spirit of this one who was to die, and that God would sustain each of them in love and bind them closer together as a family in the difficult days ahead. And we offered thanks that this one who was to die would still be with them in the power of God's love.

Such a moment leaves us with theological questions. Our understanding of grace is not relativistic. We know, with sorrow, that not all people are open to grace. If we are honest, we know that we, ourselves, often are not. Can God's grace be present, unexpectedly, in a time of prayer with a Muslim family? Is this not at least an experiencing together of God's prevenient grace? John Wesley certainly believed that God's grace is extended to all.

We cannot know where God will lead us as a church in the years ahead. We can be very certain that we will be led into deep places of human need and that the gift of God's grace is going to be there for us to share *wherever* we are led.

Chapter Two

THE GIFT
OF INCLUSIVENESS

s I look out on my congregation on a typical Sunday morning, I see many different kinds of people. While this local church is predominantly Caucasian in racial makeup, the presence of persons of other races is considerably more than token. And while most of those who come to Foundry Church are United States citizens, there are many persons from other countries here as well—some as visitors, some as permanent residents in this country. You have to look more closely and know the people more intimately to be aware that the congregation includes great economic, social, educational, and occupational diversity. We're also pretty diverse in political viewpoint, attitude toward public issues, and theological orientation, along with other points of difference. In the "church growth" movement it is sometimes alleged as high principle that a church must be homogeneous to grow, but I disagree, based on our experience. We relish our diversity; we are strengthened by it.

In that, we are but one local expression of a gift given to and through United Methodism. This is a diverse, inclusive denomination. Sometimes that causes us problems; more often it contributes to our vitality.

The Struggle for Inclusiveness

This was not always true. Within the memory of some older members of the Foundry congregation, this venerable church was virtually a segregated institution. I do not know that persons of racial minorities were actually forbidden entrance to the church for worship, but they were made to feel unwelcome. Prior to the Civil War, persons of African descent (whether slave or free) were members, but so relegated to isolated seating and secondary status that numbers of them felt constrained to leave this church to found a church of their own. That congregation, Asbury United Methodist Church, continues to thrive. We grieve over the causes of the separation but rejoice over the ministry we share in downtown Washington.

This local story is an encapsulation of the denomination's history. In the beginning, John Wesley and the early Methodists and the early Evangelicals and Brethren Christians were firmly set against slavery. Wesley himself encouraged and influenced the British struggle against the slave trade, and the earliest Methodist conferences in this country flatly forbade Methodists to own slaves. The church came to tolerate slaveholding in the slave states as more and more slaveholders were attracted to Methodism and more and more Methodists acquired slaves. Late in the eighteenth century the principle had become compromised. (Even the deeply committed Christian layman who gave the money to found my congregation in 1814—himself also a close friend of the denomination's first bishop, Francis Asbury—was a slaveholder. A *kind* slaveholder, by the standards of his time, perhaps; but a slaveholder all the same!) The denomination became embroiled in the abolitionist controversy, breaking apart in 1844 into Northern and Southern sections, only to reunite in 1939. Even after the Civil War brought emancipation to the slaves, it was not long before segregation became fixed in law and custom, within as well as beyond the church.

And the church, along with the rest of American society, had to struggle to overcome it, as it still has to struggle to overcome its effects.

Despite the awful aspects of this story, the fact that this history brought people of different races into the church meant that as we struggled to overcome racism and segregation, we found ourselves drawn into the incredible beauty and vitalities of inclusiveness. Racial inclusiveness, out of such a background, could only contribute to inclusiveness of other kinds.

There has never been a time when this denomination and its predecessors did not have both men and women members, but through most of its history it had a fixed principle that women should be subservient to men, and not permitted to become ordained ministers. That barrier was finally broken in Methodism in 1956, after a long struggle. Even after 1956 it was nearly a generation before substantial numbers of women became candidates for ordination. When I first became a seminary professor in 1966 there were only five or six women in the preordination degree program; today, in that same seminary, they number a bit more than half. In light of the splendid leadership of large numbers of ordained women, including now several bishops, we wonder how the church could ever have neglected such a treasury of gifts. It may be worthy of special note that the United Brethren churches got to this point much earlier (before the end of the nineteenth century) and that conservative Christians often gave the earliest real leadership.

Greater inclusiveness has drawn the church in this century into a struggle over affirmative action. Faced with a history of deep discrimination, was it enough simply to drop the barriers and let nature take its course? The church's instinct was to want to nudge nature along. When the legal barriers against women and minorities fell, the church chose to make special efforts to ensure the selection of some of its leaders from among those who had previously experienced discrimination—to be sure that "nature taking its course" would not mean continued bypassing of such persons. The struggle has not always been pleasant. But its fruits are plain to see in the gift of inclusiveness throughout the denomination. We have known, at least at some instinctive level, that the Holy Spirit cannot really be present unless there is a place at the table for everybody. We can't really say yet that our level of achievement corresponds to the God-given possibilities. But there has been enough movement to give us a real sense of what a gift it is to be a genuinely inclusive church.

Inclusiveness and the Future of Community

Inclusiveness is a gift through which our whole society can gain much. Just as the tragic division of the church and its compromise with slavery contributed to a bloody civil war, so the church's positive experiences with inclusiveness (and with many of its ventures in affirmative action) can help lead the broader society at these points. I do not want to make exaggerated claims here. The church has even lagged behind some aspects of the wider society. Nevertheless, the church can model a dimension of inclusiveness denied to most other parts of the culture.

Within the church, mutual acceptance contributes to greater sensitivity to old wounds and present hurt. Let me illustrate that in respect to one of the really divisive issues we still face—that of our attitude toward persons of different sexual orientation. This is an area in which honest differences make dialogue difficult. But even in the midst of its ongoing struggle over what to make of this, morally and theologically, the church is coming to a significant realization: the *personhood* of people with homosexual orientation is a sacred trust from God. The inclusion of such persons within the church, as the Body of Christ, can no longer be treated as negotiable. In our better moments we are drawn to see that

God's grace is there for all of us, and we all need it, and we cannot be self-righteous in comparing ourselves with others.

As I write these words, the church looks out on a world in which there is so much division, self-righteousness, inherited animosities between nationalities and ethnic groups, some of it centuries-old. No continent is spared. Even religion becomes the banner under which groups of people express their fear and contempt for one another. I do not wish to overstate the point. But is such division not all too real in the world as we conclude one century and enter the next?

Imperfect though it be, a church's inclusiveness is a wonderful and badly needed model of what human community can become. After experiencing worship and other aspects of our life together in an inclusive church, we are changed people when we go out into the world again. And the world outside, when given a glimpse of how extraordinary such a fellowship of diverse people can be, is challenged to look at itself in new ways. Most people find examples of warm community life attractive, but such examples can be particularly compelling if they cut across recognizable lines of division in society. How remarkable, we are led to say, that people can love one another despite such differences.

Can Secular Society Become Community?

Is it too much to expect the "world" beyond the church to be community? The church, according to many Christian thinkers, can be a foretaste of the eschatological community—the community that will be created by God through Christ at the end of time. There is some truth in this, to be sure. As long as the world is made up of sinners, there will be sinful divisions among us. Said Luther, "The world and the masses are, and always will be, unchristian, although they are all baptized and are nominally Christian." If he could write that of sixteenth-century Europe, where most people were indeed nominally Christian, how much more that must be true of a twentieth- and twenty-first-century world in which barely a third of the people are even nominally Christian! Is there really any basis for inclusiveness and community in such a splintered, secular, sinful world?

Two things can be said. First, sin and divisiveness are there in the church as well as in the world beyond the church. So, as we find the grace to overcome divisions within the church and to become a genuinely caring community, we are also helping God prove that it can happen everywhere. Second, the action of God is not limited to the churches. God is God everywhere. God is already at work in every heart. That is at least true of what we referred to in the first chapter as "prevenient grace," the grace that prepares us for Jesus Christ. St. Augustine (A.D. 354-430) had an interesting way of putting this. According to him, God creates in us a deep dissatisfaction with life until we can find ourselves in God. As his great prayer puts it, "Thou hast made us for Thyself, and our hearts are restless until they find their rest in Thee." Or as he puts it elsewhere, "You have placed salt on our tongues that we might thirst after you."

Translated into the question of inclusiveness, we can say that God has already placed within every human heart a deep dissatisfaction with the separated life. We are not happy—we cannot be happy—when we are alienated from our sisters and brothers.

Can there be such a thing as real community in the wider society of which we are but a small part? So long as sin exists, we shall have to be content with the partial realization of community. Even in the family and the church, we experience only in relative and limited form what God intends. Moreover, we cannot *make* it happen. God has to do that. But we can be confident that community is God's intention for us. God has created us with a powerful drive toward overcoming our alienation from one another. The gift of inclusiveness, a specific part of the United Methodist legacy, can become a force in the hands of God for the drawing together of humankind. At our best, we have learned that most of the diversities of background and experience, of youth and age, of specific gifts and inclinations are an enrichment to all of us. Can we not contribute this sense of gift to the rest of the world?

It may not be given to us to know how this will all work itself out in the next century. No doubt there will always be "warm animosities" and long legacies of bitterness between peoples and groups. But God's grace, experienced in the gifts of love across all the divisions, has its own magic.

The world will not be able to evade the problems posed by its religious, national, and ethnic diversities. Human differences will either be experienced as a gift to all of us or they will assuredly be destructive. That they are already. As we conclude this most bloody of all human centuries, the threat of world war has receded, but in its stead we confront a rebirth of old antagonisms. Can the bitterness never end? Can there not be generosity of spirit and forgiveness for ancient quarrels?

We may wonder about that, but we should not be surprised. In a book written just before his death, Martin Luther King Jr. asked (in the book's title), *Where Do We Go from Here: Chaos or Community?* It seems that it has to be one or the other; it cannot be in-between. Until people find it possible to value those who are different and those whom they consider enemies, the only possible answer is chaos. In the late-twentieth century, the hatred has been so deep in some places as to cause new outbreaks of genocide ("ethnic cleansing" in Bosnia; mass killing in Rwanda). Deep divisions, threatening King's "chaos," have been present on each of the continents. That is the world situation.

That does not *have* to be the world situation! The fact that churches, including The United Methodist Church, have been able to overcome deep division is foretaste and promise of what God can do for all humanity. It may appear to be an uphill struggle, but it is not only a human achievement to be pursued; inclusiveness is God's gift to be claimed and lived.

Chapter Three

THE GIFT
OF ORGANIZATION

*O*ur basic gifts are spiritual, but anybody sizing up The United Methodist Church would instantly recognize its penchant for careful organization. It is one of the banes and blessings of our existence. More blessing than bane, I think (for reasons I shall explore), but let us acknowledge frankly that organizational tidiness can suffocate as well as liberate, and can be an idol if valued for its own sake. Wesley would have agreed.

United Methodism's
Well-Organized History

That said, Wesley was in fact an organizational genius. Bear in mind that in the early years Methodism was not a "denomination," as we use the term. It was a movement among people who were nominally a part of parishes throughout the established Church of England. Wesley took the vast outpouring of spirit and energy of the movement and gave it institutional structure. The Methodists were expected to be baptized into and receive communion from parish churches, but the heart of Wesley's structure was the "class meeting." Initially, the organizational structure was to provide face-to-face settings in which the Methodists could be known and loved and held accountable by one another for their service to Christ. The class meetings were small cell groups of about a dozen people. They met weekly in homes with their class leaders. In turn, the class leaders received training and had meetings. Increasingly the movement involved lay preachers who received training and supervision from Wesley himself and were gathered annually for conferences. Those who did this work full-time were appointed to their responsibilities by Wesley.

The structure, as it evolved, was not particularly democratic except, perhaps, in the sense that everybody could be heard. In evaluating this from a contemporary perspective, we need to remember that most of the early Methodists were neither well-educated nor experienced in organization. The movement was a first opportunity for many to begin to acquire organizational skills. In any event, the structure combined the strengths of broad institutional connections—the "Conference"—with the intimacy of the class setting in which each person's own spiritual journey was valued and nurtured. That combination of organization at the broadest and the most intimate levels provided for stability and growth. People might first be attracted to the movement through great revival preaching, often out-of-doors; then they would be drawn into a class meeting where their participation could be solidified into enduring commitment.

The situation in America was a bit different. Here population was much more scattered on the frontier. Except for a few churches in the small cities of the thirteen colonies, early American Methodism was distinctly rural. Circuit riding preachers, some barely educated, made contact with isolated farms and hamlets.

American Methodism developed denominational identity during and immediately following the Revolutionary War. In some respects, that war precipitated the formation of a distinct denomination. John Wesley wrote an open letter to American colonists appealing to them to abandon their rebelliousness, and the American Methodists felt constrained to distance themselves from their founder so they wouldn't be considered Tories. They separated themselves from the British Methodists and, in 1784, with John Wesley's approval, formally organized The Methodist Episcopal Church. Denominational identity may have been inevitable in the North American setting anyway, quite apart from Wesley's political views. There was no one established church for the thirteen American colonies. Religious pluralism was inevitable in view of the different spiritual roots of the many streams of people settling the new nation. The only question was how the different denominations would be organized.

In the case of Methodism, Wesley's conference system continued, though with adaptations to the much larger and more sparsely populated territory of North America. A General Conference became the governing body for the whole church, with regional conferences meeting annually (called "annual conferences"). Beginning in 1784, American Methodism adopted the office of bishop, though Wesley seems to have been disgusted by their use of the term "bishop." Bishops were empowered to appoint clergy to their charges, to preside over the annual conferences, and to provide general oversight. In time, presiding elders or district superintendents were added to serve as administrators of districts under the supervision of the bishops. Initially the conferences were comprised entirely of clergy; in time, as the church became more democratic, laypeople were also admitted to membership. Major struggles marked the denomination's history with schisms and reunions too numerous and complicated to detail here. But, despite the struggles of an eventful history, and notwithstanding refinements and reforms along the way, the basic structure has remained essentially intact.

It is worth noting that from a purely administrative stand-point even the merger of the Methodist and Evangelical United Brethren churches in 1968 was not a particularly abrupt event for either denomination. By historical accident, the structures of the two denominations were very similar. It seems that Philip William Otterbein, principal founder of the United Brethren in Christ, and Francis Asbury, one of the first two Methodist bishops, were friends and consulted with each other on matters of church organization. At the very beginning, these two denominational streams developed very similar forms of church discipline.

Distinctive Marks of United Methodist Organization

It is remarkable that United Methodism, despite the vast changes of more than two centuries of American history, remains so similar in organization to its beginnings, and that the fundamentals of its organization have permitted important reforms and innovations to be incorporated along the way. It still is governed by a tightly organized *Book of Discipline*, incorporating foundational theological principles, a constitution, and rules of procedure governing virtually all aspects of the church's life. Ultimate authority under the constitution remains vested in the General Conference. Bishops, though now elected by regional jurisdictional conferences, are elected for life (though with a mandatory retirement age from active duty). They continue to exercise appointive power over the ordained clergy, with the normal provision that each ordained minister will receive an appointment and every church will be served by a pastor (though not necessarily by a full-time or fully ordained pastor).

Despite the tensions built into such an organizational scheme, the basic structure helps focus great organizational power in strategic ways. For instance, the resources of the whole denomination are brought to bear for the undergirding of the local church. In many instances, local churches owe their initial beginnings to funds and strategic leadership derived from the denomination. As the basic "cell" of the community of faith, the local church can count on the provision of pastoral leadership and other resources with denomination-wide forms of "quality control." While the local church is largely structured on democratic lines—with virtually all offices elected by the local church's charge conference—there is enough denominationally determined structure to ensure that a given power group within the church cannot undermine its basic character as a United Methodist church or secede from the denomination. This makes a local United Methodist church less vulnerable to the effects of demagoguery than the local churches of some other denominations.

The local church often finds its own resources joined more effectively with others in the broader mission of the denomination. Through apportioned giving, every church participates in outreach missions far beyond its own limited means. Throughout its history, the denomination has succeeded in quite remarkable ventures of faith and mission because it could count on the focused resources of a connectional system. In the nineteenth century, dozens of colleges and universities were founded through united Methodist action, and missions flourished in the advancing frontier of America and in targeted territories across the world. Mission enterprises in the twentieth century came to include a much wider agenda of issues and problems, but the fundamental connectional structure continued to focus the attention and resources of many local churches collectively.

I am not sure how well the balance between the local and the connectional in United Methodism is understood. The church is more than a collection of local congregations; there is a sense in which the whole is greater than the sum of its parts. At the same time, the local congregation is still the basic unit of the wider whole. To many United Methodists, the church *is* the local congregation, pure and simple, and "apportionments" (the fair share of contributions expected from each congregation for connectional missions, programs, and administrative costs) are sometimes viewed as an imposition for which no benefit is received. This, of course, is exactly the attitude that many people take toward public taxes! Occasionally it will be proposed that the whole system of apportionments be abandoned or cut back sharply so that all missional giving beyond the local church will be voluntary. Much giving by United Methodists *is* voluntary in that sense, of course. But to abandon the apportionment system would change more than the system of church finance. It would abandon the unique gift of United Methodism to be both local and connectional, and with it the recognition that we are members not only of a local church but of a denomination with a worldwide mission. Thus far, at least, the finely crafted balance between local and connectional has made the whole church much stronger, both locally and connectionally. This is not to say that the crafting of the balance should always remain the same. New occasions teach new duties. The church's sociological base and the mission needs it confronts have changed dramatically through the years. But the fundamental understanding that we are both connectional and local has not.

Is United Methodist Organization Democratic?

In his own way, John Wesley may have been more democratic than appearances suggest. He certainly respected the unique gifts of all of the people, even the lowliest, and his conferences made provision for different voices to be heard. At the same time, he admittedly ran a fairly tight ship. There was never much room for doubt as to who was ultimately in charge!

Most Methodist denominations in the world are vastly more democratic today. Bishops have always had great power in United Methodism and its predecessor denominations, but they have had to be elected first to exercise it. They have had to exercise their power within policy frameworks established by the elected and delegated General Conference and, with respect to many policy questions, the annual conferences. It is interesting to observe the bishops at General Conference. They take turns presiding over this body, but otherwise they are seated as observers on the platform, unable to speak unless specifically invited to do so. Bishops are the one category of United Methodist membership who, by definition, cannot be elected to serve in the General Conference. Although the conferences initially were made up entirely of clergy, for more than a century they have been half clergy and half laity. With the admission of women to full voting rights and to the right of ordination, the sexist limitation upon democracy disappeared decades ago. So the church is substantially democratic.

But not entirely. The fact that half the members of an annual conference and half the delegates to a General Conference are ordained clergy means that the fifty thousand ordained clergy have equal representation at all levels with more than eight million laity. Is that democratic?

Perhaps not. But church government is different from civil government at this point: In its basic theological character it is more than an expression of the feelings and desires of its members. It is a part of what Paul called the Body of Christ. It must therefore balance in some way the deep traditions of faithfulness with the more immediate perceptions and wishes of its people. In the long run, these cannot be in serious conflict or the church would disintegrate. But in preserving the balance, serious provision must be made for the continued faithfulness of the church to its formative traditions. Later we will consider the balancing of received traditions with current experience. But here we must not forget that even in the government of the church a more than casual reflection of the church's traditions must be present. How does this affect our understanding of democracy in church government?

The Meaning of Ordination

To answer that question we must consider the meaning of ordination more closely. Here we confront another anomaly: important though ordination obviously is, The United Methodist Church has had a terrible time coming up with a generally accepted doctrine of ordination. General Conference after General Conference, the church has delegated to commissions and task forces the responsibility of proposing a definitive understanding. But each time, the end result has been more frustration. Why is this so? I do not believe it is because the various task forces and commissions have been incompetent or irresponsible; rather, it may be because of a built-in conflict that cannot easily be resolved.

On the one hand, ordination confers sacramental authority consistent with long traditions of priesthood. United Methodism, though it has made no effort to preserve traditions of apostolic succession and though from the beginning it did not regard the office of bishop as a separate order, still preserves much in the understanding of ordination that it inherited from the Anglicanism of John Wesley's day. On the other hand, United Methodism is a distinctly Protestant form of Christianity, which means that it insists upon the priesthood of all believers. The church emphasizes that every baptized Christian is a "minister," and not only those who are specifically ordained. The General Conference of 1988, for instance, specified that the simple term "minister" should never be used when one means "ordained minister," for all Christians are "ministers."

Being ordained *seems* to make a difference, but does it *really*? Clearly, the church's theology no longer embraces the notion that the sacraments of baptism and Eucharist have some ontological effect when performed by an ordained person that would be lacking if performed by a lay Christian. No special "magic" is to be imputed to United Methodist ordination! Yet, we believe something special is in fact there. What is it?

A partial answer may at least be contained in the recent tendency to describe ordination as a "representative" ministry. The word can be taken in two senses. The ordained minister is representative of Christ and representative of the church as a whole. Lay Christians can properly protest that they, too, are called to represent Christ. But when someone is ordained, the implication is there that the church has assessed that person's "call" and confirmed it. The church is satisfied that that person (1) sufficiently represents the faith of the church, (2) can articulate that faith sufficiently well not to mislead others about the meaning of that faith, (3) has adequate skills to fulfill the offices normally entrusted to ordained ministers, and (4) in character and spirit, personally embodies or models what a Christian should be perceived to be. This is a tall order, of course, and nobody fully represents all this. Yet, is this not what the church's general membership expects of its clergy? And when somebody is identified as a United Methodist ordained minister, is it not true that non-United Methodists expect this person to reflect the basic character of the denomination dependably? It is difficult to state such an understanding of ordination with precision, and that may be good. For whatever United Methodists intend by ordination, they do not mean that there are two classes of Christians, the ordained and nonordained.

Nevertheless, the idea of representative ministry may help us understand why the proportionately heavier "weighting" of clergy participation in annual and General conferences is not necessarily as undemocratic as it might seem. The clergy have themselves already gone through a much more exacting process of being "elected." Their ability to represent the deep meaning of this community of faith has already been put to the test, and their gifts and skills must be sufficiently present to ensure that the church will not change its basic course without being fully aware of the implications.

The Authority of Bishops

If ordination poses difficulties for United Methodism, the episcopacy may present even greater ones. Unlike Roman Catholicism, Anglicanism, and Eastern Orthodoxy, United Methodism does not ordain bishops as bishops. Bishops are ordained elders, like all other ordained elders except that they have been *elected* to the office of general superintendency in the church. No doubt, in the process of election to episcopacy care is taken by conscientious electors (delegates to the jurisdictional conferences, where bishops are elected) to be certain that those elected to this high office really do represent the whole church. But they do not have a differently defined theological function. In this, their authority is considerably less than, say, that of an Anglican or Episcopalian bishop. Yet in the exercise of institutional power—particularly in the direct appointment of all other ordained elders to their responsibilities—United Methodist bishops have considerably more actual authority than the bishops of most other denominations.

From time to time the proposal has been made that bishops should be elected to specified terms so that this power will be more accountable to the whole church (which was the pattern of the former Evangelical United Brethren denomination). Formally, it is possible to remove a bishop from office before the mandatory retirement age; actually, that is nearly impossible except in cases of serious misbehavior. Bishops are assigned to their respective geographical areas by a committee of laity and clergy at the jurisdictional level, and that is one point at which some accountability is exercised. But it remains true that most bishops, once elected by a particular set of electors at a particular time and place, remain empowered until the time of retirement. The best defense of what may appear to be an undemocratic power structure in the life of the church would be somewhat similar to our discussion of ordination. Probably the most searching questions have to do with whether there is enough accountability in this structure and whether the power itself is too great.

I predict that the church will return to such questions from time to time and that future evolution will be in the direction of an episcopacy with greater theological weight and less sheer institutional power, or that there will come a time when episcopal election will be for limited, but renewable, terms of service.

Church Bureaucracy

Conferences, clergy, and bishops are not the only points in the life of the denomination where power is located. Like every denomination, United Methodism has bureaucratic organizations to give effect to its programs and missions at regional, national, and global levels. Bureaucracy is often maligned in the church as well as in the secular world. My first experience at a General Conference was in the 1952 meeting in San Francisco, which I attended as a visitor during my student days. The big, visible issue at the conference was whether the bureaucracy had got out of hand and needed serious reform. In fact, a good deal of restructuring occurred at that General Conference and at a number of subsequent General Conferences.

Unresponsiveness (or even arrogance) can creep into every organization of officials charged with duties and powers, and church bureaucracies are no exception. At the same time, the absolute necessity of such organizations can be forgotten by lay Christians. What aspect of civilized life does not depend upon bureaucratic organization to a considerable degree? Here, as elsewhere, the key questions are the relative ones: How much? Of what kind? For what purposes?

I offer no sweeping judgments about the current and future shape of United Methodist bureaucracies, but I do venture three cautions.

First, the church should be careful as it balances organizational competencies against theological purpose. It is a mistake to import organizational models derived from other realms (such as business, education, or government) without carefully assessing them theologically. It may be possible to achieve secular effectiveness (for instance, in fund-raising) while undercutting the church's basic character as the Body of Christ in mission to the world.

Second, bureaucracies often require specific forms of expertise that must be acquired through education and experience. Personnel policies must therefore be crafted with care, with due regard for organizational leadership as a valid and necessary form of Christian ministry.

Third, fundamental changes in organizational structure should be undertaken with care and not for symbolic reasons. If a "message" needs to be sent to the "bureaucrats," it is far better to do it directly and responsibly.

The Promise of United Methodist Organization

Evidently this denomination's organizational gifts remain useful. The fact that the fundamentals have served so well through more than two centuries of abruptly changing circumstances suggests that John Wesley's organizational genius lives on. The peculiarly United Methodist models would not serve every denomination equally well. But, that point accepted, the church's attempt to balance faithfulness to its traditions with expanding democracy is promising. And the effort to hold the local and the connectional in a creative tension speaks to a fundamental problem in all civilized life, both within and beyond the churches. The church, of all communities, must be especially careful that its organizational accomplishments not be made ends in themselves. When United Methodists have taken that point to heart, their organizational structures have served impressively.

Chapter Four

THE GIFT OF
THOUGHTFUL FAITH

*U*nited Methodism, by tradition and inclination, has never been a "confessional" church in the sense of some other denominations. It does not seek to elaborate creedal statements, the particulars of which must be embraced without question by all faithful members. It is not that the church takes an "anything goes" attitude toward matters of theological conviction. From the time of Wesley and Otterbein, this church has had convictions. But it has generally understood its convictions to transcend their abstract formulation. "If my heart is as your heart," said Wesley, "give me your hand."

What I find fascinating about the history and present character of the church is that it could so wholeheartedly embrace the life of the spirit, letting that burst forth in spontaneous song and pious worship and benevolent good works, and at the same time have such respect for the intellectual life. In one of Charles Wesley's hymns the lines appear, "unite the pair so long disjoined, knowledge and vital piety; learning and holiness combined, and truth and love let all men see." It hasn't always been easy. But from the beginning, both have been present. The Wesleys and a few of the other early Methodist leaders were highly trained in the best

British university traditions—and they preached enthusiastically and warmly to unlettered masses. In nineteenth-century America, poorly educated circuit riding preachers conducted their camp meetings and revivals with vast outpourings of feelings; and the churches they formed promptly organized, on the expanding American frontier, dozens of colleges and universities. In time, theological seminaries appeared and the denomination's educational standards for its clergy were upgraded. The Methodists created the first denominational publishing house in America for books and church school literature. Methodists were expected to use their minds.

Why Does It Matter?

Does it really matter whether Christians think about their faith? Certainly Christian faith is not an intellectual game, nor do we regard highly educated and theologically sophisticated people as better Christians than the simple and untutored. There are many saintly Christians who are not as well equipped intellectually as others but who, spiritually, far outshine those who are more gifted intellectually and better educated. Even so, those who have lesser intellectual gifts must still use them to full capacity. We are admonished to worship God with our mind as well as our heart and soul. If we do not, our faith will be fragmentary. It will reflect only a specialized part of us, the "spiritual" or "religious" part. We need our mind in order to integrate our whole life in accordance with our faith.

Another way to put this is that if we cannot believe that our faith is *true*, it cannot integrate our lives. We can pretend to believe certain things (even pretend to ourselves), but belief cannot be forced. The problem arises when the contents of our faith are in conflict with other things we believe. It is possible, at least for a time, to put the different forms of belief in separate compartments. But then our faith ceases to be a unifying "worldview" for us. We hold it only as a fragment.

When our faith is challenged by any aspect of our experience, we have to think it through. Either we will succeed in integrating the new experience into our overall faith perspective or our faith will be weakened, perhaps even abandoned altogether. Suppose we gain new scientific information that challenges long-held beliefs. If the scientific information is convincing, then we will have to struggle to a new, perhaps deeper level of understanding of our faith. This does not have to be a threat to faith. Indeed, faith can be strengthened, not weakened, by the challenge. It will certainly be tested. Similarly, a formative, deeply emotional religious experience or a sudden loss of relationship can trigger questions about the loving nature of God. These, too, must be integrated into the whole life.

Some of the most challenging problems center on our reverence for and use of the Bible. The problem was stated during a General Conference debate some years ago (1988) when a lay delegate voiced his sadness that his early Sunday school training had not prepared him to think critically: "It took me almost fifty years to free myself up from what I was taught in Sunday school by honest, good people who were Bible teachers but not Bible students." If the impression is left that a good Christian will accept *everything* in the Bible as factually true, then how is one to deal with the inconsistencies and the direct conflicts with well-known truths about the natural world? For instance, could the sun literally have stood still while Joshua fought against the Amorites? How can the stories of creation, taken literally, be squared with incontestable evidences of science with which they are in conflict? The struggle to overcome such conflicts can, if pursued honestly, lead to deeper understanding of biblical faith, but not without the use of one's mind!

Sometimes we discover great truth through the telling and retelling of the ancient biblical stories, even when the details are exaggerated or not factually accurate. For instance, the story of Adam and Eve in the Garden of Eden (in Genesis 2–3) conveys important insights into the human condition that can be grasped and accepted even by people who also accept scientific accounts of the origins of humankind. We balk at characterizing any aspect of the Bible as "myth." But that is mostly because we think of a myth as something that is untrue. We need to take a second look. Myths often contain the deeper truths.

The gravest intellectual problems may not be those posed by science. After all, a scientific worldview is based on faith in our minds' ability to understand basic principles governing the universe. While that is not the same thing as religious faith, it is not inconsistent with belief in a universe created by a rational God. Indisputable conclusions of science may not be consistent with naive views of the Bible, but they may be consistent with more profound beliefs that are biblical. Deeper challenges are posed by the problem of evil. How can the Christian understanding of God's power and God's love be squared with the persistence of suffering, injustice, and death? The struggle to understand that is both a challenge to our minds—as we sort through specific issues—and also to our ability to trust beyond what we can see.

The Quadrilateral

Such problems are not unique to United Methodism, but this denomination has been gifted with a promising way to deal with them. Through the Wesleyan "quadrilateral," the denomination has developed a more rounded way of thinking about theological truth. (Though each of the four parts of the quadrilateral was used creatively by John Wesley, it remained for the late Albert Outler and other twentieth-century United Methodist theologians to work this out sys-

tematically.) According to this, the Bible, tradition, experience, and reason are all important in arriving at theological
truth.

The Bible, as constitutive expression of the faith, is pri-
mary. It is understood to be authoritative witness to the
Word of God. Many United Methodists would say that the
Bible *is* the "Word of God," not that it is *witness to* the Word.
The reason for speaking of it as witness to the Word is that
God's actual communication with humanity has occurred
before the setting forth in writing. Article II of the traditional
"Articles of Religion" speaks of "The Son, who is the Word
of the Father," and Article V notes that "The Holy Scripture
containeth all things necessary to salvation." Such language
does not identify all of the Bible as literally God's words. To
Christians, God's communication is preeminently through
Jesus Christ. As the Gospel of John puts this, "the Word
(*Logos*) became flesh and lived among us, and we have seen
his glory, the glory as of a father's only son, full of grace and
truth" (John 1:14). The Bible was written over a long period
of time. Even the New Testament was composed over a
period of decades. God's action came first. Indeed, the one
important thing we have that the New Testament church did
not have is the New Testament itself! But both the Old and
New Testaments are the primary written expressions of
God's covenant with humanity. We always come back to
them to get our grounding.

What does biblical *authority* mean, then, to United Methodists? Many believe that the biblical words are themselves
a direct communication from God and that the Bible is un-
erringly true, both spiritually and factually. I suspect that a
fairly large majority of United Methodists are not biblical
literalists in that sense. (For what it may be worth, a study
conducted among Methodists in 1959 found only slightly
more than 8 percent who agreed that "every word [of the
Bible] is true because it came directly from God." A study of
United Methodists today might yield a similar result.) The

problem with the more literalistic view of biblical authority is that it leaves us with a unidimensional Bible—all of it on one level, confronted as an external authority, not as an authority from within. The deeper appropriation of the Bible occurs when we, in common with the Reformers, read the Bible "in the Spirit." It is not necessary for every aspect of the Bible to speak to us in the same way, nor is it necessary for us to have to struggle unduly over inconsistencies within the Bible and conflicts between some biblical accounts and generally acknowledged facts about ancient history and the natural world. The other three aspects of the quadrilateral help us with this.

There is tradition, for instance. There is a broad sense in which the Bible is itself a part of Christian tradition. But when the quadrilateral refers to "tradition," it refers to all of the traditions beyond the Bible: other theological writings, stories of saints and martyrs, the formulations of great church councils, evolving liturgical practices, hymns. Such traditions have great formative weight. In most cases, a direct line can be traced between Scripture and tradition, but tradition is not simply the explication of the meaning of Scripture. The doctrine of the Trinity, for instance, is not outlined as such in Scripture (though it does appear as a brief baptismal formula in Matthew 28:19); but early Christian liturgies used trinitarian language, and early Christian thinkers found the Trinity a very helpful way to understand the faith. The conception found favor among second-century Christians and was, in due course, given more authoritative status by the Council of Nicaea in A.D. 325. Tradition is not opposed to Scripture, of course, but postbiblical traditions select aspects of biblical teaching that the church, over time, has found to be more central.

This all points to the importance of experience. By this, the quadrilateral means both personal and corporate experience. Experience is not simply subjective: it includes the subject. United Methodists have always placed high emphasis upon spiritual experience, beginning at least with John Wesley's own experiencing of a heart "strangely warmed." There is a danger here, in that subjective experience can stray far from Bible and tradition, thus losing its moorings in the faith. As part of the quadrilateral, experience must be considered in terms of Bible and tradition. By the same token, unless Bible and tradition connect with experience, they cannot be authoritative for the believer. They must be brought into the context of our personal experience. Perhaps this part of the quadrilateral means that external authority cannot be re-garded as authoritative as long as it remains external.

The fourth component is reason. The quadrilateral, by including reason, recognizes the importance of theological thought. Scripture, tradition, and experience must be drawn together coherently. And by noting the role of reason, the quadrilateral encompasses and recognizes other forms of knowledge as well.

The quadrilateral is not a precise formula for theological truth-seeking. It may rather assure that theological truth never finds complete closure, since each of the three extra-biblical sources of theological thought is continually devel-oping. That may be disquieting, particularly for people who want the security of final truth in fixed, recognizable, and enforceable form. But that has never been the United Meth-odist style. United Methodism, on the whole, would rather risk temporary error than permanent barriers to new truth. God always has something new to say, and United Meth-odists want to be able to listen.

Partly for such reasons, United Methodism has not taken readily to theological loyalty oaths—at least not beyond a few central commitments—nor to broad inquiries into the possible heresy of fellow Christians. This does not mean that the concept of heresy is foreign; it does mean that United Methodists have confidence in the power of positive witness through the Holy Spirit.

The general stance is occasionally put to the test. Movements are started, responding to what their leaders take to be doctrinal crises in the life of the church. Declarations are circulated calling upon the faithful to resist theological errors threatening to engulf the church. One such, published in 1995, denied "the claim that the individual is free to decide what is true and what is false, what is good and what is evil." It rejected (a bit over-dramatically, I think) "widespread and often unchallenged practices in and by the Church that rebel against the Lordship of Jesus Christ."

No doubt, there has never been a time when rebellion against the Lordship of Jesus Christ has been absent among us, and within us, for we are all sinners. No doubt it will continue to be important for church leadership to clarify the distinction between what is clearly true and what is clearly false. But when we drift into regarding such boundary maintenance as the main task of Christian thought, we make it more difficult for God to speak to us in fresh ways. If the faith is reduced to objective thought forms that can be identified and protected, it no longer is a grateful response to God's grace. Faith is not so much assent to certain propositions as it is response to God's love. Thoughtfulness is important, but the openness and balance represented by the quadrilateral serves truth better than codified propositions to be accepted or rejected.

This openness and balance is not the same as theological relativism or subjectivism. There is such a thing as truth, even absolute truth. But the absolute is God, not particular thought forms about God. The absolute God is present to us in Jesus Christ, in the work of creation, in the Holy Spirit, but we cannot claim to know everything about God. In faithfulness, we must be prepared for God to do a new thing. Scripture and the great moments of tradition, including the early formative Christian councils, express central aspects of our faith. But they are not the only word. So, also, we cannot dispense with the importance of our own experience and that of the church. The denial that "the individual is free to decide what is true and what is false, what is good and what is evil" is only part of the picture. Of course, as this statement recognizes, truth is not a personal invention, for God is objectively real. But we must not obscure the importance of our own personal encounter with truth. It is meaningless to pretend to accept as true, on some external authority, what does not commend itself to us as true. I must add to this that those who insist most upon certain defined propositions as the faith once and for all delivered generally have too much confidence in their own ability to discern that faith in its entirety—and too little openness to the possibility that God can yet speak to them through the voices of those who disagree.

The various versions of "feminist theology" help to illustrate the point. Considered by some to be a genuine threat to essential Christian teaching, this movement in fact appears in various forms. Every form of feminist theology with which I am familiar stands opposed to exclusively patriarchal conceptions of Christian faith—whether that means the symbolization of God in exclusively masculine terms, the use of male terminology in reference to both women and men (as in general use of male pronouns when both genders are intended), and dominance of men over women in priestly and church governmental roles. Such patriarchal usages are so deeply ingrained in Christian scripture and tradition that the feminist challenge is easily portrayed as heretical or even pagan. Indeed, some forms of feminist theology may be "outside the pale." That is true on the face of it of the theology of Mary Daly, who considers Christian faith to be so essentially patriarchal as to be unredeemable, and who has therefore explicitly abandoned Christianity. That may also be true with versions of feminist theology that seek to replace an exclusively masculine understanding of God with an exclusively feminine understanding. Some forms of feminist theology can best be described as ambiguous in their efforts to avoid patriarchal imagery, which usually means simply that more needs to be said.

But it is well to look to the main point. Is feminist theology right in challenging the dominance of masculine symbolizations of God and masculine leadership in the church? By allowing both experience and reason to play a role in the church's theological discourse, Christians are challenged to understand God more deeply. Personal language for God (such as the *abba* or "papa" terminology used by Jesus and Paul) helps convey the deep truth that God is not impersonal. God is not just a force or a process; God is not an abstraction. God is deeply personal, like a good human father. But if we go the further step and say that God is more like a father than like a mother, more masculine than feminine—as much tradition would lead us to do—then it just could be that God is challenging us in this day to think in larger terms. Personal, yes; masculine, not necessarily. God certainly is neither male nor female *physically*! The first Article of Religion says that "there is but one living and true God, everlasting, *without body or parts* . . . " (my emphasis). The source of all creation is not any kind of physical being; God transcends the physical realm. Nor can we say that what we take to be masculine attributes are grounded in the divine life in a way that feminine attributes are not. Feminist theology helps open this up for new inspection. Though theologians have always understood that human language, being drawn from human experience, never fully encompasses the meaning of God, feminist theology has helped make us all more sensitive to that truth.

What is at stake in this theological tendency is not only the adequacy of our conceptual formulations. It is whether we really do consider women and men to be equal and whether the full creative energies and possibilities of women will be valued and used alongside those of men. When God is seen only in masculine terms it is difficult to evade the implication that God is more *like* men than women. Has not much Christian tradition embraced that implication?

Jesus Christ represents a different question. To deny Jesus' maleness is to obscure the importance of the Incarnation. To be a person, Jesus had to be some specific kind of person, and he was, in fact, a male person. But his being male and not female in the Incarnation should not be given theological weight, as if maleness expresses full humanity in some way that femaleness does not. Thus, those branches of the Christian church that have resisted inclusion of women in ministry or priesthood on the grounds that Jesus was male and not female elevate the accidental to the essential. Could we not as easily say that since Jesus was a Jew only persons of Jewish background should be ordained ministers or priests? Or that only carpenters need apply?

We may be certain that feminist issues in theology will continue to occupy the church for some time. It seems to me that the characteristic United Methodist approach of the quadrilateral is much more useful in working through those issues than a more rigidly "confessional" stance that might easily confuse the essential with what is peripheral. We are in a better position to learn and to grow. Can we protect ourselves sufficiently against real error? Serious theological error may have roots that are more spiritual than intellectual. The church's great stake in theological orthodoxy is in the spiritual direction toward which it points. When, for instance, we speak—as we should—about the primacy of Christ for all Christian theology, it is the reality of Christ as a redemptive channel of God's grace, communicated especially on the cross and confirmed through resurrection, that matters. It is quite possible, and not at all infrequent, that we hear all the right words about this conveyed in a spirit that denies the words. On the other hand, ill-chosen words, not well thought through, can be uttered by faithful Christians whose hearts are absolutely on the right track. The greater flexibilities of our quadrilateral, with its invitation to dialogue and mutual growth in comprehending the faith, can better draw heart and mind together than confessional rigidities.

These words are not written to encourage either anti-intellectualism or theological relativism, except the form of anti-intellectualism that recognizes that God is greater than our intellects and the relativism that acknowledges that all human grasp of theological truth is relative to the one absolute, God, who exceeds all we can know.

Karl Barth (never one to be crippled by theological uncertainties!) wrote of the dangers of allowing theology to be locked into some past construction:

> "Confessions" exist in order that we may go through them (not once but continually), but not that we should return to them, take up our abode in them, and conduct our further thinking from their standpoint and in bondage to them. The Church never did well to attach itself stubbornly to one man—whether his name was Thomas, . . . or Luther, or Calvin—and in his school to attach itself to one form of its doctrine. And it was never at any time good for it to look back instead of forwards as a matter of principle, as if accepting a "realized eschatology," as if not believing in the coming Lord. (*Church Dogmatics,* volume III, book 4, p. xiii)

I suspect Barth would not have been wholly comfortable with the quadrilateral, but his words are in its spirit.

Thoughtfulness in an Era of Competing Absolutisms

This is not an easy period for Christians who resist the spirit of fanaticism and theological intimidation. I do not think this is a matter of "left" or "right," nor even of any particular religion in contrast with others. It is an age in which many people in all parts of the world and apparently in all cultures seek the security of fixed, once-for-all answers to the timeless questions. How are differences among the contending versions of truth to be resolved? By armed struggle, or by the loudest voices, or by the greatest social pressures?

Surely the only resolutions that will matter in the long run are those afforded by thoughtful approaches of people who are open to mutually respectful dialogue. The only answers that count, ultimately, are the ones that prove persuasive. People yearn, not only for more secure moorings in faith but for a religious perspective that brings their whole life and world into plausible focus. People may settle for something less than that for the time being; in the long run they will not.

It is not a comfortable time for a mainline denomination like United Methodism to try to engage the culture with the full resources and openness of its quadrilateral. But is it not an extraordinary gift the church offers the world of the twenty-first century? The real gift, underlying the church's intellectual methodology, is that of God's grace in Jesus Christ. The methodology opens channels of communication to demonstrate the plausibility of this understanding of reality.

Will it be successful? Let us express our confidence in God by saying that it will be if it deserves to be! And let us have done with too much speculation about what is or is not the "wave of the future." Peter Berger, the sociologist-theologian, spoke to this persuasively in his book, *A Rumor of Angels* (Garden City, N.Y.: Doubleday, 1969):

> It is only human to be exhilarated if one thinks one is riding on the crest of the future. All too often, however, such exhilaration gives way to the sobering recognition that what looked like a mighty wave of history was only a marginal eddy in

the stream of events. . . . Theology must begin and end with
the question of truth. (122-123)

United Methodism cannot pretend to have a corner on
truth. Its gift, in that respect, may be to acknowledge that
nobody does.

Chapter Five

THE GIFT
OF EVANGELISM

*U*nited Methodists and their spiritual forebears have always been "evangelical" as that term is understood by Christians. We are what we are because of the "good news" of God's love, most fully revealed in Christ. We respond to the good news by sharing it with others.

The Wesleyan revival was evangelistic through and through. After their own conversion experiences, the early Methodist leaders felt a compelling drive to reach out to others with the good news. Their preaching brought the gospel to thousands of people, whom they then drew into small communities of faith and mutual support and accountability. The same was true of the early preachers of The Evangelical United Brethren Church. John Seybert, one of that church's early nineteenth-century circuit riders exemplified both United Brethren and Methodist evangelistic zeal:

> In 1834 over an eleven month period he held seven "Big Meetings" (all-day evangelistic efforts often lasting into the night, and of two to three day duration), five camp meetings, traveled 4,406 miles on horseback, visited many families to pray with them, preached three hundred times. . . . In his

round of duties no place was too far, no hour too late, no effort too great for him to counsel with a person or to preach to a gathering or to a congregation, in the interest of reaching souls for Christ's kingdom. (Raymond M. Veh, "John Seybert: Symbol of a Passion," unpublished paper, 1986)

Such evangelistic efforts were commonplace among early Methodist as well as Brethren circuit riders. We may feel remote from that, today, but that extraordinary evangelistic effort is what made our United Methodist Church possible.

Theologically, this gift of evangelism was an expression of God's grace in Jesus Christ, but from the beginning there was a distinctive twist. It was the combination of "justifying" and "sanctifying" grace. The first was the bold announcement to people who had given up all hope that God had accepted them, setting aside their unworthiness. They were invited to respond in the spirit of an evangelical Anglican hymn of the early nineteenth century: "Just as I am, without one plea, but that thy blood was shed for me, and that thou bidst me come to thee." Justifying grace is the grace that accepts us just as we are, just when we think ourselves unacceptable. But the Methodist and United Brethren twist was to combine this with sanctifying grace—the grace that leads us toward perfection in love, that helps us overcome the power of sin in our lives. The Charles Wesley hymn that supplies the title to this book expresses the spirit of sanctifying grace: "A charge to keep I have, a God to glorify, a never-dying soul to save, and fit it for the sky."

It is extremely difficult, though very important, to combine these two! If we emphasize justification alone we may invite complacency. If we speak only of sanctification, it is an invitation to salvation by "works." The combination of justifying and sanctifying grace begins in the total, unqualified love of God and grows through our response to what God has done. The evangelistic appeal growing out of this com-bination is twofold. It is first a proclamation of God's un-merited love for us. That is the "good news," pure and simple. It is second an invitation to a life fulfilled in that love.

Evangelism, in the historic Methodist and Brethren sense, has thus involved both a proclamation of what God, through Christ, has done, and a call for decision. God has decided for us, but now we have to decide whether to accept that gift and live by it—or live into it, as we might better say, since the dead weight of our sin can seldom if ever be overcome in a moment.

This twofold understanding of grace also means that evangelism can never be exclusively a "spiritual" or personal matter. Sanctifying grace summons us into a life of love in a world of people. Salvation is not solely a spiritual transaction between ourselves and God. It is our call to respond to the lordship of Christ in the world. That has its beginning in justifying grace, but it cannot end there. So evangelism is also a call to discipleship.

Although the martyred German theologian Dietrich Bon-hoeffer was Lutheran, not Methodist, his understanding of justifying grace and discipleship seems very similar. Cau-tioning us against what he called "cheap grace," Bonhoeffer put the call to discipleship in the strongest terms: "When Christ calls a man, he bids him come and die." That is not the language usually employed by evangelists, though the early Methodists often spoke of dying to sin—and sin was not simply an abstraction. When we are "called to die" it is to renounce everything in our lives and in our world that stands in the way of God's love.

The current baptismal liturgy of The United Methodist Church includes questions suggesting the importance of both justifying and sanctifying grace: "Do you renounce the spiritual forces of wickedness, reject the evil powers of this world, and repent of your sin? Do you accept the freedom and power God gives you to resist evil, injustice, and oppression in whatever forms they present themselves? Do you confess Jesus Christ as your Savior, put your whole trust in his grace, and promise to serve him as your Lord, in union with the church which Christ has opened to people of all ages, nations, and races?" These are the right questions, though something could be said for placing the question about trust in the grace of Jesus Christ first, for justification precedes sanctification.

Varieties of Evangelism

A persistent problem with evangelism in the United Methodist tradition has been a tendency to romanticize the way it was conducted during the periods of most rapid growth. That is quite understandable. What worked before might work again. But Methodism grew by leaps and bounds during the American frontier era when circuit-riding preachers and camp meetings were highly successful. We must learn from the past, but it can be a mistake to follow it slavishly. It would be difficult to emulate Wesley's open-air preaching successfully. On the other hand, television may today open up new opportunities Wesley could not have imagined; I can visualize John Wesley wondering why United Methodists of this era have done relatively little with that. In any era, direct sharing of the faith with individuals will be important.

The most meaningful sharing is not usually with strangers. Sometimes it has been in the church school, in confirmation classes, in youth camps where young people are invited to make a commitment of their lives to the one who has given them their lives. Sometimes it has been in the bosom of a loving Christian family, in such fashion that there never occurs a single moment of crisis, but rather a growing maturation in the faith. In each case there is a deep conviction of God's love and a wholehearted commitment of one's life in return. Imperfections persist, but the direction of life is secure.

In my mind's eye, I can readily identify people in my own congregation who illustrate very different versions of this growing maturation in the faith. We have children and youth who seem clearly on the way. I am impressed by their growing sense of God's work in their own lives and their growing sensitivity toward others. They give themselves wholeheartedly to service projects for poor people, and I am moved when I see them interacting in loving ways with those whom they are serving. I am not aware of many of them undergoing sharp, life-defining crises. But I see personal decisions being made for lives of service, based upon and illustrating both justifying and sanctifying grace (though not generally with self-conscious reference to these words).

We also have people whose lives have been broken, including alcoholics, people who have been abused, people who have been abusers, people whose marriages have collapsed, people who have felt rejected, people who have despaired of any further possibilities for their lives. Sometimes they have come to the church through the low-key witnessing or simple invitation of friends, sometimes they have just wandered in, thinking there might be some possibilities here. And then something "clicked" and God became real. Not infrequently, these people will speak of a genuine crisis in their lives and how they have been wholly transformed. From a "pastor's eye" viewpoint there is much evidence that they have been. In some cases such people have become the very backbone of the leadership of the church.

Evangelistic Campaigns

Drawing upon the church's evangelical legacies, efforts have been mounted from time to time to reach the unchurched through specific campaigns. Often these have been inspired by romantic conceptions of what worked in some previous era. "If we would only return to the evangelistic fervor of the original Methodists or those who made the church grow a hundred years ago." Sometimes particular numerical goals have been adopted—as when the church, in General Conference assembled in 1984, solemnly covenanted to double the church's membership by the year 2000.

I do not wish to denigrate the evangelical concern—that is a part of the gift of United Methodism that is to be celebrated. It is clear that vast numbers of lonely, despairing, broken lives need exactly what the gospel has to offer and that the church has been at its best when it has sought out such people. But several points must be made.

First, as we have said, the spiritual heart of Methodist evangelism has always been grace. God truly loves us in spite of the sin and imperfection in our lives. When Christians place further conditions on this, including criteria drawn from current attitudes of social respectability, that comes across as further rejection. "Successful" evangelism throughout history (and not only Methodist history) has often, maybe even usually, been among people who felt themselves to be outcast. There are very large numbers of people in urban American society who feel themselves to be outcast, for various reasons. A church that is genuinely interested in proclaiming the gospel of God's grace to such persons will certainly achieve results.

Second, the mechanisms of evangelistic campaigns can get in the way. Numerical quotas, training in communication techniques possibly owing more to business sales experience than to the church's own experience, slick advertising materials—such mechanisms can be distancing when what is needed is more on the heart-to-heart level.

Third, almost inevitably evangelistic campaigns come across more as mechanisms of church growth for its own sake than as efforts to help people connect with God and, on a deep spiritual level, with one another. But the church's institutional success is not necessarily the same as evangelism. A church that is faithful to the gospel may, in fact and for that reason, go through periods in which it is *losing* members. The great Dutch theologian Hendrik Kraemer is alleged to have given an unexpected answer when asked how the churches of Europe were doing at the end of the Second World War. Oh, he is supposed to have said, the church is doing much better—attendance is down! The story may be apocryphal, but it makes the point. Not everything that appears a success externally reflects the transforming power of God's grace in the lives of people. Kraemer doubtless had reference to the tragic capitulation of so much of the prewar church to the blandishments of Hitler's Nazism. While, for a time, that increased church attendance and prosperity, it was very far removed from the gospel.

Evangelism and the Church

Still, there is no particular virtue in loss of members. Some membership loss in the United States is a simple reflection of demographic trends. For instance, it is not too surprising that a denomination with many churches in rural areas might be losing members in proportion to the population losses of those areas. But I suspect that more churches fail to gain members because they are not quite ready to reach out to everybody.

Real evangelism connects people to the church. Televangelism that leaves people sitting in their living rooms is not life-transforming. To be changed by the gospel is also to be incorporated into a community of faith in which one can gain ongoing reinforcement and through which one can serve. When somebody says "I am a spiritual Christian even though I do not belong to the church," we may ask how deep the spirituality really runs. The early Wesleyans did not content themselves with the outdoor preaching; they connected people with one another in the Methodist societies. That is as necessary today.

I am intrigued by efforts to recapture the essence of the early Methodist class meetings through covenant-discipleship groups. They are a reminder that it is important for every Christian to be connected with other Christians on a face-to-face level. That point is particularly important in a large congregation where new members can easily become more or less anonymous spectators. If they find the spectacle compelling enough, such people may be faithful in attendance, but their Christian experience will be truncated and their faithfulness will not be dependable. Large churches can maintain vitality only if their members find meaningful smaller group connections within the larger congregation. Within The United Methodist Church the *DISCIPLE* studies program has been quite helpful, and the new covenant-discipleship groups may be as well. They will need to avoid appearances of elitism, as though the "real" Christian disciples are the ones who sign up for them, and their procedures of mutual accountability must not substitute such "works" for the grace by which we are saved.

The Promise of United Methodist Evangelism

The world needs more, not less, evangelism. I am continually surprised that the people in my congregation whom I consider to be most evangelistic are ones who shy away from the very word! Here is a woman whom I recruited to serve on a reconstituted evangelism committee who wondered whether we shouldn't find a different word. She is personally responsible for the presence of many people in our church, and she is engaged in mission outreach activities of various kinds. What was her problem with the word *evangelism*?

I'm certain it was the connotation of the word: it has come to be associated with manipulative techniques, religious Fundamentalism, and reactionary politics. Of course, she knows that these are only caricatures of real evangelism, for the proclamation of God's good news is bigger than that. The great Australian Methodist evangelist Sir Alan Walker speaks of evangelism as "the whole gospel for the whole world." The whole gospel redirects every aspect of life through God's grace, toward concern for the whole world. Real evangelism challenges us to abandon self-centeredness; it does not require us to sacrifice intellectual integrity. Real evangelism is concerned for individual persons; it does not ask us to abandon social responsibility and the requirements of social justice. Real evangelism draws together all of the other gifts referred to in this book, focusing them upon our outreach to people whose lives have been broken—and upon our nurturing of people, young and old, who are already present in the community of faith.

The world of the first century A.D. proved to be very fertile soil for the proclamation of the gospel. At first a trickle, then a flood of people heard the message and responded gladly. We do not have to romanticize that period or the faithfulness of those Christians, sinners then as now, to see truly astounding results. What of the world as we enter a third millennium? Vast numbers of people clearly need exactly the gospel of grace and redirection that the church has to bring. If we are to deliver it effectively, our conception of evangelism has to be big enough and free enough from cultural captivities. The large test is whether United Methodism can continue to grasp that evangelism is both social and individual by nature, and that it has to do with both this world and the world to come.

A deep recovery of the gift of evangelism will require a renewed recognition that evangelism is what the church is about in all of its being and doing. It is not a specialized activity, all by itself, that some Christians may engage in while others may not. But if we are to understand that, we must also recognize the great diversity of ways in which the good news of God's love must be communicated in a confused, pluralistic, and conflicted world.

Chapter Six

THE GIFT OF
SOCIAL WITNESS

*A*ny preacher who ventures to speak on the great issues of the day from the pulpit is sure to be told, sooner or later, that preaching should be limited to more personal or "spiritual" concerns. Occasionally I have received communications to that effect. One of my favorites was a letter from a visitor who objected to my dealing with specific "policy options" when there were national leaders present in the congregation. He went on to say, however, that "the earlier part of the sermon, when dealing with the exegesis of Isaiah and the theology of Barth, was interesting and sufficiently remote from the current choices facing the country." I'm not sure that I dealt at all well with the issues in question—which had to do with world peace. But I was intrigued by the implication that a sermon should be "sufficiently remote from the current issues facing the country." Should the church be silent about such things?

United Methodism's Legacy of Social Witness

Part of the gift of United Methodism is a long legacy of disregarding that tempting advice. Beginning with John Wesley and continuing in England and on the American frontier, the church has continually challenged injustice and championed social reform. It has, in the light of history, sometimes been mistaken. But its social witness has at least conveyed the message that the gospel is social as well as personal and that the "spiritual" cannot be detached from the actual earthly existence of real human beings.

Sometimes a distinction is made between the "personal" gospel and a "social" gospel. John Wesley would have been offended by that. To him, it is all one gospel. He lived well before the age of social science; even economics could scarcely be said to have begun, although Adam Smith's *The Wealth of Nations* was published when Wesley was 74. Wesley knew nothing of the Social Gospel movement. Still, he did have a keen sense of how economic forces affect human well-being, and in his struggle to understand the roots of economic distress we can see something of the spirit of the later Social Gospel movement. He was deeply opposed to the institution of slavery and encouraged those who, through political action, sought to bring an end to the slave trade. Although not a pacifist, he was no stranger to the evils and futilities of war. Wesley did not think of social, economic, political conditions themselves as the essence of the gospel; yet he did have a keen sense that social institutions and practices enhance or diminish God's purposes for human existence. Note, for instance, Wesley's compassionate response to the plight of poor people, obviously based on his own, direct pastoral contact:

> I have known those who could afford to eat a little coarse food once every other day. I have known one in London (and one that a few years before had all the conveniences of life) picking up from a dunghill stinking sprats, and carrying them home for herself and her children. I have known another gathering the bones which the dogs had left in the streets, and making broth of them, to prolong a wretched life. (John Wesley, "Thoughts on the Present Scarcity of Provi-

sion," in George W. Forell, ed., *Christian Social Teachings* [Garden City, N.Y.: Doubleday, 1960], 286)

Social concern, though less active at some times, has never disappeared among Wesley's spiritual descendants. Methodists were active participants in the North American abolitionist movement. Methodists were largely responsible for some other reforms, including the abolition of dueling as a way for "gentlemen" to settle their disputes. (A nineteenth-century pastor of the congregation I serve, by virtue of his preaching and his role as a congressional chaplain, deserves much credit for that reform.) Methodists were active in the nineteenth- as well as twentieth-century feminist movements. Methodist leadership had much to do with the nation's experiment with prohibition in the early twentieth century. I am among those who feel that the latter was not a wise reform, although the motives behind it reflected deep human concern for the actual effects of alcohol upon persons and families and communities.

Social Christianity in America was given enormous impetus by what came to be called the Social Gospel movement. In its first expression, that movement is usually dated by historians from the end of the Civil War in 1865 to the beginning of World War I around 1914. It coincided with the great burst of industrialism in this country, and it was principally concerned about the human wretchedness experienced by many industrial workers and their families. Methodism cannot claim credit for initiating the Social Gospel movement itself. That movement received earlier leadership from Baptists, Congregationalists, Unitarians, and Episcopalians. In the early years of the twentieth century, however, Methodists became increasingly active. A group of five young Methodist leaders founded the Methodist Federation for Social Service in 1907 and proposed a "Social Creed" for adoption by the 1908 General Conference of The Methodist Episcopal Church. The creed was approved not only by that General Conference but by the newly formed Federal Council of Churches as an ecumenical statement. Frank Mason North, one of the five authors of the Social Creed, wrote the hymn "Where Cross the Crowded Ways of Life," which exemplified the spirit of the Social Gospel movement.

From the first decade of the twentieth century onward, Methodist leadership was important to that movement. Bishop Francis J. McConnell helped lead the church into a positive relationship with the labor movement. Bishop G. Bromley Oxnam similarly supported economic empowerment for working people and, late in his life, helped bring an end to McCarthyism in post–World War II America. Theological leaders like Walter G. Mueder and L. Harold DeWolf took activist positions on a variety of social issues and helped stimulate the church to be courageous in its social witness. Methodists were very active in the Civil Rights movement, the movement to end the Vietnam War, and many other causes that could be described as further developments of the Social Gospel movement.

The Civil Rights movement was a particularly difficult one for the church. The Methodist Church had been deeply compromised by the creation of a segregated ecclesial structure in 1939, when nearly three hundred thousand African Americans were relegated to racially defined annual conferences in a segregated jurisdiction. The battle over that was an internal struggle paralleling the battle over segregation in the larger society. Those who advocated full racial integration had to face the charge that their reform movement was not an expression of the spiritual gospel and the threat that their efforts could split the church. One can only wonder what the church would have been if those advocating change had not persisted. As recently as 1950 a study showed that fewer than two hundred predominantly white Methodist churches in the country included African Americans; as recently as 1958 two of the denomination's theological seminaries remained officially segregated; in the early 1960s distinguished biracial groups were turned away from the door or even arrested while seeking to attend some southern churches. This has not been an easy struggle, nor has it been limited to the American South.

And yet, the successes of the struggle—incomplete though they continue to be—are now cause for celebration among United Methodists of all racial groups in all parts of the country. The church was willing to deal with reform within its own life lent greater integrity to its social witness in the wider society. And United Methodists did "weigh in" in the Civil Rights movement alongside persons from other denominations and secular organizations.

The Church's Social Teaching

Beginning early in the twentieth century, the adoption of statements and resolutions was increasingly common in Methodist annual and general conferences. The Social Creed itself, begun modestly as a brief statement dealing mainly with labor issues, evolved over time into a much more lengthy and detailed document setting forth the church's social principles. (What is now called the "Social Creed" is a liturgical summary of the statement of social principles.) From a simple page-long creed in 1908, the church has developed a volume of over six hundred pages of social principles and resolutions.

The various resolutions and statements reflect different levels of competence in grappling with problems and their theological implications. Some have been very thoughtfully researched and formulated while others seem to have been written in haste. The activist Methodist spirit is usually present. Even when the denomination has proved to be wrong, the willingness to tackle hard questions has conveyed the view that the issues should matter to Christians as Christians. It is better to risk error—and sometimes fall into it—than to avoid mistakes by remaining disengaged. The latter would be the biggest mistake of all, conveying that Christian faith is altogether otherworldly. Still, there is no virtue in being wrong. It is a legitimate complaint that all too often the vast collection of statements and resolutions has not been preceded by serious study and theological reflection. People may honor the church for its courage in tackling hard questions, but statements that do not reflect careful thought and study cannot command the world's respect. The great moments in the church's social witness have been those in which moral fervor has been expressed with intellectual integrity.

Two such moments were supplied by the Council of Bishops. Their "Crusade for a New World Order" during World War II attempted to enlist popular support for United States participation in a permanent United Nations organization. The drive included writings, speeches at large services and rallies, letters to public figures. In retrospect one might conclude that the movement was not as deep theologically as it might have been. But it spoke a relevant word in a timely way, and it made a difference.

The other such moment was the 1985 Bishops' pastoral letter "In Defense of Creation." This thoughtful, nearly book-length document sets forth reasons why the church and nation should renounce nuclear war. Drawing upon both pacifist and "just war" moral traditions, the document noted that the case against nuclear war could be made with either. While the pastoral was criticized—sometimes roundly—it had the kind of thoughtfulness and weight that is needed to evoke wide-ranging discussion of the issues.

Both these initiatives, along with a number of others emanating from the General Conference, have helped people frame public issues in light of Christian faith. An ideal form of social witness does not simply announce conclusions; it invites the reader into a thought process. It is needed in the public arena, of all places, because it helps remind all participants in the great debates that ultimately what we do as a community should be an expression of our values. Debates often center on narrower interests. Sometimes we think we are being "pragmatic." However, what is pragmatic or practical is not only a common sense or technical question; it is also a question of the values we want to put into practice. What is practical from one point of view may not be from another if the values underlying the conflicting viewpoints are very different. The church's contribution to public debate is to challenge people to think more broadly about the public good and to be more honest about the values they are ultimately espousing.

The church's traditions of social witness are a gift to the broader society even at points where that witness has been rejected.

Grounding Social Doctrine Theologically

A sampling of the vast array of resolutions and statements on social issues leads to the conclusion that the church has been fairly casual in relating its theological convictions to the issues of the day. Sometimes the "biblical-theological" basis of conclusions is quite perfunctory; sometimes it seems that the theological preface is supplied afterward to preserve appearances, and that no serious struggle is experienced. This undercuts the very purpose of the church's social witness, which is to help people see the relationship between their formative values and their views on public issues.

I wish the church would spend more time with the broad questions of social doctrine, perhaps thinking through the theological meaning of a whole sphere of life. What is politics to the Christian? Economics? Sexuality? Some of the United Methodist "Social Principles" and resolutions do this, at least up to a point. Where they do, it is much easier for the reader to grasp *why* particular positions have subsequently been taken. This is to be contrasted with the use of biblical "proof texts"—i.e., the use of particular verses of Scripture to justify particular positions. The latter implies that all biblical texts are normative, and that we should feel bound by any and every isolated Bible verse. The church's theological tradition is not to take the Bible in such a unidimensional way. We also consult tradition, we are influenced by our own and the church's faith experience, and we use our God-given capacity to reason. Carefully articulated social doctrine helps us frame the theological debate over social issues so that we can at least disagree with one another more intelligently.

Prior to the 1992 General Conference, a small group of theologians (myself included) sought to clarify what we took to be a confused pattern of thought in the church's Social Principles on issues of war and peace. On the one hand, the Social Principles state quite flatly that "war is incompatible with the teachings and example of Christ," and continue "we therefore reject war as an instrument of national foreign policy and insist that the first moral duty of all nations is to resolve by peaceful means every dispute that arises between or among them." In another passage, the Social Principles reject "coercion, violence, and war" as "incompatible with the gospel and spirit of Christ." Taken at face value, that would appear to commit The United Methodist Church to pacifism. That is an honorable position, to be sure, with much Christian precedent behind it. But the Social Principles also affirm that "persons and groups must feel secure in their life" and that "nations, too, must feel secure in the world if world community is to become a fact." And, while the Social Principles offer moral support to conscientious objectors, the document affirms that "we also support and extend the Church's ministry to those persons who conscientiously choose to serve the armed forces or to accept alternative service."

Most United Methodists, including those who are pacifists, would not classify The United Methodist Church as one of the pacifist denominations. But the pattern of statements in the Social Principles leaves a confused picture. The theologians offered a clarifying amendment acknowledging frankly that some United Methodists stand in the pacifist tradition while others are more persuaded by the "just war" tradition in which military action can be accepted as a last resort if certain moral standards have been met. Such a statement could help clarify the reasons why different members, in good faith, take different positions. Pursued in depth, such a statement could seek to illuminate how the Christian doctrines of sin and grace affect our judgments, as Christians, about the uses of coercion. Pacifists can argue that social coercion only exacerbates the effects of sin: better to be committed to nonviolence so that the message of God's grace can come through human love in unambiguous form. Nonpacifists can respond that the reality of sin will always lead to injustice unless there are specific mechanisms to hold it in check, preserving space in which grace can do its work. Both views can be expressed with theological depth. In the church's teaching on war and peace and on criminal justice it is helpful to keep both traditions before us.

Similar things could be said about other church statements on social issues. We cannot be content to state our conclusions; our contributions to the public debate need to be framed as deeply as possible out of our core beliefs. Sometimes we do this reasonably well, sometimes not so well.

Social Witness Facing an Uncertain Future

The church cannot speak to every issue (though a casual look at *The Book of Resolutions* might suggest that we really try!). In our choice of issues we do well to look to the ones that have enduring significance and to frame them in such a way that people of good faith and intellectual honesty can find real help. On some issues we can already speak with a strong consensus. For example, United Methodists everywhere are strongly opposed to gambling, whether as a way of enhancing public revenues or as public "recreation." We are pretty clear in our opposition to pornography, to violence in the mass media, to sexual promiscuity and abuse. We understand, now, that racism is a sin and that all forms of racial discrimination are to be resisted within and beyond the church. On these, and a variety of other questions, we can speak with a nearly united voice. There are other issues we must struggle with as we seek to know God's will in an imperfect world.

I want to lift out two of the issues I consider especially important, both of them subject to continuing debate within the church.

The Church's Teaching on Homosexuality

The first is the ongoing debate within and beyond the church over homosexuality. The divisiveness of the issue undermines our ability as a church to address other issues. The issue is also important because homosexual persons are probably the most stigmatized group in the country, and our attitude toward such people affects the way we perceive all those who are viewed with contempt.

A "given" in the debate is that, while the Bible has comparatively little to say about homosexuality, what it does say is almost uniformly negative (there are about seven such statements in the Old and New Testaments). Similarly, insofar as Christian thought through the centuries has engaged this issue, it has generally been in condemnation of homosexuals. So the specific teachings of Scripture and tradition on this subject are generally opposed to homosexual practice. The issue surfaced in American churches during the 1960s and 1970s with the emergence of a gay and lesbian rights movement, which has led to greater assertiveness on the part of homosexual persons and a backlash from those who reject their position. In The United Methodist Church, the issue was hotly contested at the 1972 General Conference with the adoption, in the new Social Principles, of the statement: "We do not condone the practice of homosexuality and consider this practice incompatible with Christian teaching." More recent General Conferences have struggled with this issue, with some modification of language and a more direct advocacy of the civil rights of homosexual persons, but continue to state that the practice of homosexuality is "incompatible with Christian teaching." The issue has been polarizing in many of the denominations and in the wider society. If United Methodism could find more creative ways to deal with it that would be a real gift within and beyond the church.

I am not sure that we can, but it would at least be a step in the right direction for people to struggle over the basis for the positions they take. On the one hand, those who find homosexual practice to be incompatible with Christian teaching must go beyond simply citing proof texts from the six or seven biblical passages that mention homosexuality—unless they are willing to argue *every* social issue on that basis. For instance, we could not say that the specific condemnation of homosexual practice in Leviticus 20 or Romans 1 is an adequate basis, unless we are also willing to condemn women for speaking in church on the basis of I Corinthians 14 or I Timothy 2 (or, for that matter, unless one is willing to put homosexuals to death on the basis of Leviticus 20!).

On the other hand, those wishing to liberalize the church's teaching must be more cautious about scientific evidence that some persons are born homosexuals. At the present time the scientific data are suggestive but unclear. We are not certain why some people are homosexual and others are not, though it does seem clear that many homosexual persons have experienced themselves as "different" in that respect since early childhood. Both sides do well to ponder the deeper theological questions: Is homosexual practice compatible with life in grace? Can it be an expression of deeply humanizing covenantal faithfulness through which we experience God's gift of love?

If these questions are to set the standard by which we evaluate our beliefs about sexuality, the issue becomes a bit more clear. Such a standard certainly rules out exploitative or casual experiences of sexual intercourse, whether heterosexual or homosexual. But it is not clear that it excludes morally committed homosexual, as well as heterosexual, relationships. At least, if the church condemns all such homosexual relationships it should be prepared to say *why*. As I write these words I think specifically of several persons in my own congregation who have been in such committed relationships for years. Some are young, some older; some are Republicans, some Democrats; some conservative in their views of public issues, some liberal; most are successful in their vocations as lawyers, architects, businesspersons, health professionals, and so on. Most do not fit the popular stereotypes. I may not be a sufficiently discerning judge (and I am reluctant to play the role), but most give every evidence of being committed church members who take their Christian profession seriously and practice it faithfully. Several put many of us to shame with the selflessness of their mutual caring. In the three years I have served this church, not one has given offense or cause for scandal. Our congregation is one in which homosexual persons can function and contribute without stigma, but a number have had more negative experiences in their churches of origin. Those churches have missed a real gift!

Is it not time for the church at large to take this kind of evidence seriously in framing its social teaching? There is an old medical axiom, "First, do no harm." I wonder whether there shouldn't be some version of that in our moral teaching: "First, be very certain before you condemn." I know something of the weight of negative feelings toward all homosexual persons because I once shared these feelings. Perhaps what is needed now in the church's social teaching is a period during which we frankly acknowledge that the church does not have a sufficient basis either to condone or to condemn.

Would that not be the responsible position for the church to take while it allows experience to accumulate and scientific data to become more clear—and while we do our deeper theological reflecting? For a major denomination to issue a frank, and suitably modest, declaration of its inability yet to arrive at a common mind on such an explosive subject, along with its willingness to subordinate the issue to our deeper common loyalty to Christ—would that not be an extraordinary gift to give our troubled society?

The Challenge of a New World Order

The other issue is very different. The Cold War, which had dominated and defined international consciousness for forty years, suddenly came to an end at the beginning of the final decade of the twentieth century. Some people may have felt disoriented by the loss of the clearly identified enemy! For most of us it was a great relief. For all of us it brought the opportunity to see new possibilities.

The United Methodist Church has long been a committed supporter of the United Nations. Before the end of World War II, the bishops of what was then The Methodist Church had called the church to the Crusade for a New World Order, a cause in which many other denominations also enlisted. President Franklin D. Roosevelt, in one of his last letters (to Bishop G. Bromley Oxnam) credited the churches with making it politically possible for the United States to take a leadership position in support of a new world organization to replace the defunct League of Nations. Whether Roosevelt's letter was friendly hyperbole or not, there is no question that the church did become deeply committed to the new United Nations organization.

That support has continued, although the UN's basic mission of securing the blessings of peace for humanity has had mixed results. The largest frustration through the years was the Cold War. With the superpowers, the United States and the Soviet Union, armed to the teeth and possessing the nuclear capability of destroying all civilized life, the UN lacked either the will or the means to guarantee the peace. The great powers were set against each other indirectly in the two great wars of this period, and their sundry client states occasionally were involved in lesser conflicts. The UN accomplished a number of good things, including its work through the World Health Organization and UNICEF, but its peace-keeping role was frustrated.

The end of the Cold War seems to have opened a new chapter. Ironically, the era of new global possibilities is accompanied by a new wave of isolationism in the United States and some other countries. It seems difficult for many people to see the conditions of global peace as important to the national interest. Yet, what could be more important? If, for example, Russia (armed as it still is for nuclear war) were to come under totalitarian leadership again, either from the "left" or the "right," would we not bitterly repent our lack of vision—as we repent today the lack of vision of those who allowed German social and political deterioration following World War I to provide the Nazis with their opportunity? On humanitarian if not politically self-interested grounds, what are Christians to make of the continuing economic distress of many developing nations? It may no longer seem necessary to bid against the USSR for the support of these nations. Should we therefore feel that we no longer have an obligation to help them toward a better future?

The theological issue seems clear: The whole world is God's intended community. God is not a respecter of nations, even though nations have had a vocation to fulfill in the providence of God. The United Methodist Church is not located in every part of the world. But, though centered in the United States, it is a significant presence in a number of other countries as well. Its international character can be a gift of global consciousness to those countries, not least to the United States. It can be a reminder that every international conflict is also a family quarrel, within the family of human-kind; and it can challenge us to see that the distress of any part of humankind is an injury to all the rest.

As the world approaches the beginning of the third millennium, can The United Methodist Church recover and enhance its vision of a new world order?

Learning How to Disagree Creatively

These and other issues often give rise to passionate conflict. Controversy is not necessarily bad. On the contrary, it helps us grow when we confront contrary points of view. But for conflict to be creative, it needs to be conducted by people who acknowledge a higher mutual loyalty and who care about one another. On the whole, The United Methodist Church really isn't so bad at this. We have our squabbles, of course, and not just at quadrennial intervals either. But the connectional structure and the appointment system reduce the possibilities of open rupture, and the more flexible approach to theological debate helps save our disagreements from being overly invested with ultimacy. Still, a church has to keep working at it.

A church is one of the few places where one can say to a spirited opponent, "We disagree about this, but I still love you," and really mean it. It is one of the few places where we can actually pray together about our differences, and not let the prayers be disguised forms of acrimony. It is one of the few places where the lines of disagreement can shift, and we do not have to have adversarial parties and caucuses. We do have those, of course; our challenge is to keep reminding ourselves that our common loyalty to Christ and the church is prior to our provisional loyalty to a caucus.

How badly the world at large needs such a spirit. We cannot expect the world to be the church, but humanity is capable, at some level, of acknowledging fellow humanity. The prospect of civilization should be exciting to everybody, just as the realities of self-centeredness and isolation are ultimately demoralizing. We do not exist for ourselves alone. At some level, most people feel the force of that. Learning how to disagree creatively is part of the discipline of community. The late Jesuit theologian Father John Courtney Murray reminded us of two important points. First, civilization is to be defined as people "locked together in argument." By that, he did not mean acrimony. He meant people who cared greatly about issues and who respected one another's opinions enough to seek to persuade. And the second point is that "genuine disagreement is a rare achievement." It is rare because so often what appears to be disagreement is in fact only people arguing past one another. It is an achievement because a genuine disagreement is a form of mutual understanding. Perhaps it is also an achievement because genuine disagreement can be the prelude to later agreement at a higher level.

So, if the words of a Roman Catholic theologian can inspire a Protestant denomination to enhance its natural gift of social witness to humanity, let us make the most of it!

Chapter Seven

THE GIFT OF
ECUMENICAL SPIRIT

*T*he earliest Methodists must have appeared anything but ecumenical. As a movement within the Church of England, the Methodists could only have been perceived as disruptive of unity. Their strong emphasis upon "holiness," their tight organizational structure, their system of accountability, and their readiness to expel those who took their responsibilities too lightly must have come across to non-Methodists as a judgment against those not inclined to join them on their own terms.

And yet, from the time of Wesley, the Methodists had an ecumenical side to them. Methodists are fond of quoting Wesley's saying, "If your heart is as my heart, give me your hand," as evidence of that spirit. Wesley's own spiritual development was nurtured by non-Anglican sources—principally the continental pietist tradition (including the Moravians who influenced him so much during his youthful missionary venture to Georgia), Puritan and Catholic devotional literature, and even the Greek patristic writings. This is also true of Evangelicals such as Otterbein. Although the Evangelical and Brethren traditions might also appear more sectarian than ecumenical, the reality was of extraordinary openness. Commitment and discipline were expected, but the spirit of love overshadowed doctrinal precision. In such traditions, tests of orthodoxy could not take on the importance of evangelistic fervor and mutual caring.

In nineteenth-century America, ecumenism was often expressed through unofficial organizations, such as missionary societies, social cause organizations, the YMCA, the YWCA, and the Student Volunteer Movement that crossed denominational lines. Methodists like Frances Willard and John R. Mott were actively involved in these. Willard was active in feminist and temperance organizations. Mott chaired the Student Volunteer Movement and helped found the World Student Christian Federation.

Twentieth-century ecumenism received its first great impetus with the Edinburgh World Missionary Conference of 1910, which was chaired by Mott. From this conference, the Life and Work Movement, the World Missionary Council, and the Faith and Order Movement, all dealing with important aspects of ecumenical dialogue and cooperation, were to develop, with the formation of the World Council of Churches in 1948 as a major result. Methodists were deeply involved in all of this. In the United States itself, Methodism played an important role in the creation and development in 1908 of the Federal Council of Churches, an organization that was to evolve into the present National Council of Churches, with local and state councils of churches modeled along similar lines.

The various councils of churches never were intended to be superchurches. They were "federal" in principle, which means that they combined the unity of mutual respect and recognition with the continuing diversities of denominational structure. This made it possible for the denominations to address their differences through dialogue while engaging in common action where possible. Methodists have been a part of these federal ventures throughout the twentieth century.

Methodists have also participated in more direct institutional mergers. The most successful of these, from the Methodist standpoint, were the 1939 merger of The Methodist Episcopal Church, The Methodist Episcopal Church, South, and The Methodist Protestant Church to form The Methodist Church, and the 1968 merger of The Methodist Church and The Evangelical United Brethren Church to form The United Methodist Church. In the 1940s and 1950s, Methodist missionary statesman E. Stanley Jones sought to interest mainline American denominations in a form of institutional merger. That did not resonate particularly well with the targeted denominations. But, beginning in the early 1960s, Methodists and Evangelical United Brethren began to participate fully in negotiations with a number of other mainline American Protestant denominations in the Consultation on Church Union (COCU). The latter development has disappointed its more enthusiastic supporters by failing to progress more rapidly toward creation of a new, merged American denomination. Nevertheless, COCU has certainly led to specific forms of ecumenical cooperation and to greater mutual recognition and respect.

The twentieth century has been a great ecumenical period for Christianity. Looking at the century as a whole, one is much more impressed by the drive toward unity than by divisiveness and schism. There have been notable accomplishments: great ecumenical conferences, the establishment of the World Council of Churches, and regional, national, and local councils of churches, the flourishing of ecumenical expressions within broad church families—such as the World Methodist Council and the Lutheran World Federation, numbers of outright mergers of similar denominations—such as the United Methodist mergers of 1939 and 1968 and similar Presbyterian and Lutheran reunions. Beginning early in the century, Eastern Orthodoxy has been included in much of the ecumenical movement, despite serious theological and liturgical differences. Roman Catholicism held back. But by the 1960s, with the election of John XXIII to the papacy and the Second Vatican Council, that church became much more open and ecumenical.

Is twentieth-century ecumenism a passing moment in church history? Will the churches continue to seek greater unity as they witness and serve? I am reminded of the remark of a Roman Catholic bishop at the time of the Second Vatican Council. Asked by a reporter whether the progressive work of the Council would be permanent, the bishop replied that the Council had already done "irreparable good." Perhaps we may conclude similarly that the ecumenical movement of the twentieth century as a whole has done "irreparable good"!

The Ecumenical Spirit
and Legacies of Division

If that is true, no one denomination can claim credit. Each participant in the conversation has had unique gifts to bring. What have the United Methodists' gifts been, and how should United Methodists view the continuing realities of division?

This church's theological traditions have certainly had something to offer. Most United Methodist intellectual contributions are not exclusively United Methodist, but they are a gift all the same. The "quadrilateral" that we have already explored is certainly relevant to the ecumenical conversation, inviting all Christians to explore the common gifts of Scripture and tradition in the light of experience and reason. The doctrine of prevenient grace is a specific theological point at which United Methodist thought helps undergird the wider ecumenical conversation. That doctrine, by emphasizing how God's grace is at work in the lives of all people even before any encounter with Jesus Christ, helps us recognize that God's unifying work precedes ours. God is "out there" already. We must never think of other people and other groups as alien. Our stance can be more one of relating to the God who is already at work in others and less that of confronting pure, unadulterated error.

It may be, however, that United Methodism's greatest gift to the ecumenical conversation is in its spirit. To speak of an ecumenical spirit is to acknowledge that genuine ecumenicity has its foundation in spiritual encounter with God, transcending divisive theological rigidities. It is not necessary that Christians have exactly the same spiritual experience to be ecumenical, only that they recognize the authenticity of the experience of others. As we have seen, the early Methodists were able to mitigate the potential divisiveness of theological differences by seeing that life in the Spirit cannot be reduced to abstract thought. Their organizational structures might truly have been an ecumenical barrier (as, to some extent, they still are). But organization also is subordinate to life in the Spirit; it is not an end in itself, but a means to the true end. So the basis was there for ecumenical openness, even for ecumenical eagerness. United Methodists can approach other Christians with hope and confidence that we will encounter new dimensions of the life of God to enrich our own.

At the same time, this very basis of vital ecumenicity is a caution against identifying God's Spirit with organizational, liturgical, or even sacramental forms. My impression is that the greatest barriers to ecumenical unity exist precisely in differences at these levels. Much is sometimes made of doctrinal differences, and they can be quite real. But organizational differences and differences in worship practices can be more decisive.

In ecumenical conversation with Episcopalians or Anglicans, for instance, United Methodists balk at the idea that their clergy might have to be reordained by bishops who are supposed to be in apostolic succession. That appears to imply that somehow United Methodist orders are, at present, defective. In conversation with Baptists and others who practice "believer's baptism" (as opposed to infant baptism), the notion that United Methodists who were baptized as infants should be rebaptized is unacceptable. In both these illustrations, the underlying issue for United Methodists would be our unwillingness to treat such things as absolute or definitive. God's Spirit cannot be reduced to such things. Happily, recent developments in the COCU conversation partners and the remarkable ecumenical discussions of Baptism, Eucharist, and Ministry have removed most such barriers.

On the other hand, now that United Methodists fully accept and rejoice in the ordination of women, there is a substantial barrier to proceeding toward organic union with denominations that do not. Currently Roman Catholics and Orthodox Christians fall into that category, as do many Southern Baptists and other conservative Protestant denominations. The full acceptance of ordained women clergy has, for us, become a non-negotiable issue.

Few United Methodists would ascribe theological status to our conference system and system of appointments, but congregationally organized denominations would regard the imposition of such a system as oppressive—just as United Methodists, persuaded by the continued functional merits of these systems, would be reluctant to abandon them. Interestingly, the organic merger of the Methodist and Evangelical United Methodist denominations in 1964 owed more to their close organizational resemblances than to special theological affinities.

We do not know where the ecumenical movement will finally take us. The momentum toward unity is strong, its theological grounds compelling. It is unthinkable that The United Methodist Church or any of the other mainline denominations should revert to an isolated posture. It is an important sociological reality that many laypersons find it easy to move from the local churches of one denomination to those of another, without experiencing much real difference. At the local church level, the patterns of connectional

administration are scarcely visible. And, in the case of mainline churches, worship patterns are all quite similar (hymns,
prayers, sermons, scriptures). Differences within denominations can be quite as great as differences between them.

The congregation I serve may not be typical of all, but I
can report that virtually every membership class includes
persons from other denominational traditions. It is quite
normal to have persons from denominations that have significant theological differences with United Methodism—
such as Roman Catholicism and the Southern Baptist
denomination. Sometimes interdenominational couples present themselves. We have several families in which one
spouse is United Methodist and the other Roman Catholic.
Some will attend our church most of the time; others more
or less divide their attendance between our church and a
church of the other denomination, with both partners attend-
ing both churches together. That kind of practical ecumenicity has great sociological relevance to the broader
movement. Laypeople are observing that there are few differences that matter very much. And, in this, perhaps they
are unconsciously accepting John Wesley's invitation, "If my
heart is as your heart, give me your hand." In some instances,
this practical ecumenicity may mean that people are not very
deeply committed Christians, that they do not care much
about the differences because they do not care much about
the faith itself. But I'm not persuaded that that is the case.
Some of our most faithful and deeply committed members
started out somewhere else and may someday go somewhere else. I think the deeper reason is that such laypeople
are unwilling to accept the small idolatries of organizational
or liturgical practice.

The Interfaith Horizon

What about our relationship with religions other than
Christianity? Does the ecumenical spirit extend that far as

well? The interfaith horizon poses more difficult problems. On the one hand, God is God of the whole world and prevenient grace is at work everywhere. On the other hand, Christian faith makes unique claims that cannot be abandoned.

Before speaking of the latter, we need to remind ourselves of the gift of ecumenical spirit. It is a gift of God, not of our choosing. It compels us to remember that God is bigger than we are, that the ways of God "are not our ways." The Roman Catholic Church has struggled to see this point. In its "Declaration on the Relation of the Church to Non-Christian Religions," the Second Vatican Council said that "the Catholic Church rejects nothing which is true and holy in these religions. She looks with sincere respect upon those ways of conduct and of life, those rules and teachings which, though differing in many particulars from what she holds and sets forth, nevertheless often reflect a ray of that Truth which enlightens all men [and women]." Those words, and the accompanying call for intensifying dialogue between the church and non-Christian religions, represent a refreshing openness.

The United Methodist Church could be still more open on the basis of its spirit and traditions. There is no reason why United Methodists have to reject everything about other religions indiscriminately; there is every reason why we should be open to the ways in which God may be at work there as well as in our own midst. An open attitude can spare us the subtle temptation of identifying with Christianity elements from our own cultures, even when these cultural elements really have nothing to do with the faith. It can also keep us from more harmful acts, such as using our faith as a way to emphasize the political power interests of predominantly Christian countries over those of countries whose citizens are predominantly of other faith traditions.

But what about our witness to other religions? To be in dialogue with persons of other religions is to speak as well as listen. Generally we fail to listen. In learning to listen we must not forget to speak. For our gifts are treasures also to be shared.

Some of our scriptures may seem embarrassing when read in the context of interfaith dialogue. For instance, in John 14:6 we read "Jesus said to him, 'I am the way, and the truth, and the life. No one comes to the Father except through me.' " Or, in Colossians 1:15-17 we read that Christ "is the image of the invisible God, the firstborn of all creation; for in him all things in heaven and on earth were created, things visible and invisible, whether thrones or dominions or rulers or powers—all things have been created through him and for him. He himself is before all things, and in him all things hold together." How can we say this and at the same time listen to the views of those who don't believe such things about Christ *at all*?

I suppose we cannot interpret these words in a way that would exclude the possibility of God speaking to others and saving others in ways we have not imagined. But does this not take us back to the grace we discussed in chapter 1? It is the depth of God's love, revealed in Christ, that we have to share! It is not a Christ who functions for us in some altogether external way. It is a Christ who reveals the fundamental character of God to us. If Christ means to us the depth of God's love, does this not give us something to talk about in the face of any religious tendencies (within as well as beyond the church) that conflict with our own? I am not sufficiently versed in the details and nuances of any of the other world religions to criticize them with assurance. And yet, the narrow, unloving spirit of some forms of Islam, Buddhism, and Hinduism seems contrary to God as revealed in Christ. Even within Judaism, a religion with which we share much, there are some people and movements who identify the very meaning of the covenant with occupancy of the land of Israel and whose treatment of Palestinians—both Muslim and Christian—is disrespectful and unloving. Needless to say, there are equally unloving Christians. At the least, our approach to other religions should be to say that we will not settle for anything *less* than the love of God revealed in Christ! (And in saying this, we must repent of our own unloving and narrow attitudes, and devotedly hold ourselves to the same standard.)

I am not sure we need to say more or less than that in general terms. Might we find that same quality of love outside the Christian fold? We should rejoice if we do, for it is nothing less than evidence of the power of God beyond our power. And if we do, there would be nothing about it to require us to abandon the Christ who is our Lord. But other ways of life and witness to the deep love of God can enrich our own lives, even demonstrating to us dimensions of the life of Christ we have not yet seen. When Anwar Sadat, a Sunni Muslim, took his journey to Jerusalem to open new channels of communication and reconciliation, it was a shrewd and creative political act. Yet, we can believe its creativity had origins in Sadat's personal faith as a Muslim. When Mohandas K. Gandhi, a Hindu, devoted himself to the liberation of India through satyagraha—meaning "truth force," and incorporating truth, nonviolence, and self-sacrifice—he chose political instruments well-suited to the limitations of his own people and the vulnerabilities of the British occupying power. Nonetheless, we can believe his nonviolence was also principled and based, really, upon love. In his case, we know that the New Testament and the witness of New England Quakers of the last century, profoundly affected him—as did the Methodist missionary statesman, E. Stanley Jones. Can Christians not learn something about Christ from a Sadat or a Gandhi?

In this book we have had occasion to note the conflicted state of the world as we approach the third millennium. What greater gift could United Methodism offer the present age than the gift of its ecumenical spirit? That spirit is grounded in and affirms the Christ who is God's redemptive love to us. And that spirit is what is needed to break through the rigidities and defensiveness of many of the world's peoples. When United Methodists have been true to their own gift, they have been channels of reconciliation.

Chapter Eight

THE GIFT OF HOPE

Some years ago, during a period of crisis in our national life, a well-known lay theologian was addressing a college audience. He spoke of the seriousness of the world crisis and the depth of the nation's abandonment of Christian faith. It was all doom and gloom. There was no glimmer of hope in his words. During the question period, one of the students asked him, "What, then, can we do?" His measured answer: "Take a few good books and hide them away where one day they may be found." That could not have been a United Methodist speaker! At least not one standing in the traditions of the Wesleys and the Otterbeins, the Willards and the Motts and the Harknesses and the Oxnams!

Say what you will about United Methodism and its forebears, this has always been a hopeful, activist Christian community. The church's accomplishments would tell you that. People who are not hopeful do not get things done. "Work without Hope draws nectar in a sieve," wrote Coleridge. "And Hope without an object cannot live." United Methodists have lived on hope, and they have demonstrated that their hope has an object.

Wesley's great movement transformed the lives of tens of thousands, ultimately millions of people, because he and others preached with the expectation that people would respond to the message. The American frontier preachers and lay Methodists worked their hearts out in the confident faith that God would use them to change the lives of people. They built institutions, like colleges, hospitals, and settlement houses, from meager resources because they were needed and because they had a vision that it could be done. Methodists enrolled in great social causes with an expectation of success—most recently in a Civil Rights movement of truly historic significance.

In short, United Methodists have not been so persuaded of the intractable effects of original sin as to be paralyzed. The United Methodist heritage is acquainted with sin, unquestionably, and with it the realities of failure and frustration. But their inextinguishable hopefulness has saved them from lethargy and protected them from being defeated by failure.

Have I overstated the point? Almost certainly so, because United Methodism has also had its fair share of pessimists and, especially at the present time, those from whom a "discouraging word" is not infrequently heard! But I am referring to the deep tradition, the shaping character of the church, from the time of Wesley and Otterbein. That deep tradition is more given to hopefulness than to malaise.

The gift of hope is itself an aspect of the concept of grace with which I began this little book. We can be hopeful because we are confident that God's love defines who we are and who we can be. United Methodists, historically, have not spent much time bemoaning the depravity of humankind because we have been more confident of the redemptive power of God's grace. We are aware of human sinfulness. Sometimes we need to be even more aware of how sinfulness requires the creation of constraining institutions of justice. But we do not want to ascribe too much power to sin, knowing that God's power to overcome sin is the more important reality.

From the time of Wesley, those called to serve through ordained ministry have been asked the time-honored questions, "Are you going on to perfection?" and "Do you expect to be made perfect in this life?" By perfection, Wesley meant perfection in love. Do you, the question might be rephrased, trust the power of God's grace to transform you utterly and completely? I am not sure I like to have that question addressed. I was uncomfortable answering it, though answer I did, forty years ago. It seems a bit arrogant to say that one expects to be made *perfect* in this life! Still, if we understand that the subject is God's grace and not our doing, the words can be an expression of our hopefulness.

Hope for Persons

When I returned to pastoral service after many years of seminary teaching, there were not as many surprises as one might expect. After all, I had been intimately involved in local churches through those years, and I kept in close touch with former students and other pastors. Yet there was one aspect of this transition that was, if not a surprise, at least an unexpected challenge: to become well acquainted with many people of the congregation, to come to love them, and then, sometimes unexpectedly, to see them die. Like most people, I have lost loved ones and friends. But not on this scale and not with the accompanying pastoral responsibility. Immediately I sensed that the church is very different from almost any other kind of human community: we can face the realities of death, we can really grieve, we can genuinely and deeply support one another, *because we do not believe that death has the last word!* How many times I have found myself repeating with ever-deepening confidence the words of Paul: "For I am convinced that neither death, nor life . . . will be able to separate us from the love of God in Christ Jesus our Lord" (Romans 8:38-39). Our memorial services and funerals are very different from what happens in a more secular setting, precisely because of our hope. We can combine grief over our human loss with the celebration of a treasured human life, because of our faith in God's love. That is the faith and hope that undergirds everything else.

There has always been some danger that Christians will see their hope exclusively in otherworldly terms. There is the opposite danger that Christians, in order to counteract that temptation, will think of their hope solely on the worldly plane. Genuine Christian hope combines the two. When we have, in our faith and hope, settled the ultimate question, all lesser questions come into perspective as well. Those who believe that they are ultimately safe with God are able to face all the problems and questions of human existence on earth with unbounded hopefulness.

Recently I met a man living with AIDS. He related that when he was informed of this by his doctor a few years ago he had been told that he had but three months to live, and he had better get his affairs in order. For a period of years he had been alienated by the church. It had, he felt, rejected him, and he returned the favor! But somehow he had come back into the faith, and somehow he had found his trust in the healing power of God restored. So he refused to accept the prognosis and concentrated in his prayers upon God's healing grace. He is still alive; he feels good. He knows that he will die one day, though he hopes not soon. He continues to rely upon the medical profession, but his deeper lifeline is found in prayer. There is no "magic" in this. But the hope with which he greets each day is grounded in the deeper faith and hope in God.

I often find myself thinking, when I hear people voicing their anxieties about this or that little thing, why worry so much about that? God is still there. In a few years these anxieties will have evaporated one way or another. I seldom voice such thoughts, for I do not wish to mock the fears of others and, God knows, I have my anxieties and fears as well. But we do need to remind ourselves that the ultimate hope is what gets us through the little anxieties. The ultimate hope makes it possible for us to entertain lesser hopes, knowing that whether or not they are fulfilled we are still sustained. We hope for a particular job or for a promotion. We hope to be loved and for our relationships to be successful. We may hope to be married. We hope things will work out all right for our children. We hope to remain healthy or, if ill, to be restored to health. We hope to be recognized and appreciated. We hope to have friends. Such hopes are not trivial, but neither are they the ultimate ground of hope on which we stand. We can invest ourselves in such hopes because of our confidence in God. So, when we are disappointed—as sometimes we are—we are not disillusioned. Our hope in God translates into the expectation that whatever our successes or failures, God will take our best efforts and turn them into something good.

Hope for the World

As we have seen, United Methodists have often worked hard at improving the world. We have not always been right, though the church's visions have often stood the test of time. In any case, we have been surprisingly energetic about our pursuit of social objectives.

Here, again, activism has to be sustained by hope, and specific hopes by the ultimate hope. If God is not to be present at the end of history, what possible meaning could any hope within history have for us? We can ponder the fact that when people abandon their hope for the long run, they also lose their will for the short run. For a time, the Marxist movement was sustained by the devoted energy of millions of adherents, many of whom had an unshakable confidence that this was truly the wave of the future. The time came when this confidence ran out, partly because of economic failures and political reverses, partly because of disillusionment with the self-centeredness of leaders who, by definition, should have been selflessly committed to social justice. But, I suspect, the confidence ran out because it was not sustainable by an ultimate spiritual vision. In a universe ultimately based upon unthinking matter and energy, what final hope is there? Even if the Marxist version of social justice were the correct one, why would it finally matter?

By contrast, Christians have had great staying power. They are not disillusioned easily. That is partly because their realistic understanding of human sin does not lead to many illusions. But it is more deeply because their confidence in God leads them to treat every failure as but a part of an ongoing history in which God's will ultimately will prevail.

This is not the same as secular confidence in inevitable "progress." History has its regressions as well as its surges ahead. The twentieth century, invested with the hopes of so many people a hundred years ago, produced for us two great world wars, a holocaust, vast injustices and oppressions. Still, can we not discern the fulfillment as well as the disappointment of hope? The feminist movement has done remarkably well in establishing the principle of full gender equality, even though social attainment sometimes lags behind the collective conscience. The Civil Rights movement broke the back of official segregation and put racism decisively on the defensive. Economic policy in the United States and other industrialized countries established the concept of a social "safety net" and the unacceptability of malnutrition for anyone, anywhere. The environmental movement has placed pollution on the defensive everywhere. Such accomplishments seem at times imperfect and fragile—and so they are. But the hopes invested in their accomplishment were not misplaced, and Christians can see the small hopes as pieces of the great hope.

United Methodists are not the only Christians who have specific hopes for the world and energetically pursue them. But hope is an important gift United Methodists offer.

Hope for the Church

What about the church itself? In historical terms, United Methodist history is fairly brief. We have not been around for more than a fraction of the two thousand years of Christian history. Nor is it likely that The United Methodist Church, as a separate identifiable denomination, will exist throughout the next millennium—or anywhere close to that long.

But putting it this way misses the point. The purposes of United Methodism are not tied up in the endless perpetuation of this denomination or its superficial institutional successes. This is God's church before it is ours. God has used it in powerful ways. If we are faithful to God we do not need to be anxious about the church, even though most of us have moments when we are. We can be grateful for God's gifts to us through the church, responding loyally and serving faithfully. We can safely leave the fate of the church, and our own fate, in God's hands.

I want to say more. In spite of some statistical decline in membership in recent years, I believe I see new possibilities emerging. Much of the statistical decline in mainline denominations is attributable to our failure to gain the allegiance of many in the "baby boom" generation. Deaths in the older generation are not quite matched by new members of the younger generation. That, more than the departure of disgruntled members, is the central cause of our numerical decline. There is, however, some evidence of younger adults taking a new interest in the church. In part, this may be the more or less predictable tendency of adult couples to want their children to be baptized and attend Sunday school.

But I sense something deeper. The younger adults who are coming to our church in increasing numbers seem to me to be responding to the church on four levels at once. They are attracted by a vibrant worship experience, by the possibilities of inclusion in an affirming fellowship in which all are welcome, by an intellectually honest presentation of the faith that does not require them to leave their brains at the door as they come in, and by opportunities to serve and be relevant to the wider society; and each of these four elements is grounded in a faith they can affirm wholeheartedly. These levels of experience correspond so exactly to what I take to be the formative gifts of United Methodism that I cannot but believe this church will grow in its attractiveness—provided we do not face the future fearfully and defensively.

It is, in any case, a bit incongruous for deeply committed United Methodist Christians to be pessimistic about their church. After all, aren't they themselves evidence of hope? The very fact of their caring and their commitment is a vote for the future. Is it not enough to invest ourselves wholeheartedly in the life and work of the church, and leave the rest to God?

> *To serve the present age, my calling to fulfill;*
> *O may it all my powers engage to do my Master's will!*

Index

affirmative action, 27-28
Albright, Jacob, 17-18
apportionments, 37-38
Asbury, Francis, 26, 36
assurance, doctrine of, 21
Augustine, 30
authority, biblical, 51-52

Barth, Karl, 58
Berger, Peter (*A Rumor of Angels*),
  59-60
bishops, 35, 36, 39
  authority of, 42-43
Boehm, Martin, 17
Bonhoeffer, Dietrich, 63
Book of Discipline, The, 36
Book of Resolutions, The, 79
bureaucracy, 43-44

Church Dogmatics (Barth), 58
Civil Rights movement, 74-75
Cold War, 83-84
Coleridge, Samuel, 99
community
  future of, 28-29
  secular society, 29-31

Daly, Mary, 55
debate, theological, 85-86

DeWolf, L. Harold, 74
doctrine, social, 77-79

ecumenism, 87-90
evangelism, 61-64
  campaigns, 65-67
  and membership, 67-68
  promise of, 68-70
  varieties of, 64-65
experience, spiritual, 52-53

faith, 47-50

Gandhi, Mohandas K., 96
General Conference, 36, 39
  1908, 73
  1952, 43
  1972, 80-81
  1984, 66
  1988, 40, 49
  1992, 78
gifts, 9-10
grace
  justifying, 21, 62-64
  meaning of, 19-22
  prevenient, 21, 30, 90
  promise of, 22-24
  sanctifying, 21-22, 62-64
  of United Methodism, 15-19